THE
FREEDOM
FORMULA®

"In this book, Christine Kloser beautifully explains how to integrate your spiritual nature with proven business principles to become a successful, conscious entrepreneur."

~NEALE DONALD WALSCH
Best-selling author of the *Conversations with God* series

"*The Freedom Formula* is the key to understanding the power of choice, and the process of implementing it with zeal, with passion, with heart. A must read, a great idea, a book on fire."

~MICHAEL E. GERBER
Author of *The E-Myth* and *Awakening the Entrepreneur Within*

"*The Freedom Formula* challenges entrepreneurs to think differently about their business and their quest for freedom. This must-read will guide you down a path to greater personal and professional satisfaction and lasting success."

~KENDRA TODD,
APPRENTICE WINNER
Best-selling author of *Risk & Grow Rich*, and Host of HGTV's *My House is Worth What?*

"If you're ready to make the journey of conscious entrepreneurship more smooth, effortless, easy and enjoyable, read *The Freedom Formula* and get started today."

~MARK VICTOR HANSEN
Co-creator, #1 New York Times best-selling
series *Chicken Soup for the Soul* ®
Co-author, *Cracking the Millionaire Code*
and *The One Minute Millionaire*

"Every now and then a book comes along with just the right message at just the right time. *The Freedom Formula* is one of these exceptional books."

~LORAL LANGEMEIER
Founder & CEO, Live Out Loud

"All entrepreneurs want the same thing. Freedom! Time freedom. Boss Freedom. Money freedom. Freedom to pursue their dreams. Read *The Freedom Formula* and discover the secret to experiencing freedom in your life… starting today."

~VICTORIA COLLIGAN
Founder, Ladies Who Launch

"Christine Kloser combines the heart and soul of Mother Teresa with the business savvy of successful CEOs without missing a beat. *The Freedom Formula* gives entrepreneurs both a spiritual road and a practical pathway to build lasting success."

~SUSAN HARROW
Author of *Sell Yourself Without Selling Your Soul*
and CEO of PR Secrets

"What a beautiful book! Christine Kloser has written the heart- and soul-centered business book the world has been waiting for. With clear examples and step-by-step instructions, she shows you just how to live your life's purpose and make a profit, too. Well done!"

~CHELLIE CAMPBELL,
Author of *The Wealthy Spirit* and *Zero to Zillionaire*

"Christine Kloser's new book *The Freedom Formula* is a bold step that bridges the importance of "Soul" in your business. She has woven the power of being conscious on a spiritual level with the importance of understanding how a business really works. This is a terrific piece of work for anyone who wants to operate a business on a higher spiritual level."

~JOE NUNZIATA
Best-selling author of *Spiritual Selling*

"*The Freedom Formula* is not only a practical guide to building a lifestyle business (that makes money) but it's also a kick-in-the-pants to entrepreneurs everywhere to be among the strongest and most positive influences in the new world; a world where everyone experiences real freedom."

~MICHAEL PORT
Author of *Book Yourself Solid* and *Beyond Booked Solid*

"Finally, a book for conscious entrepreneurs that explains the value of integrating your soul into your business. Christine Kloser makes it clear why advancing consciousness in business is the key to advancing consciousness worldwide — and she makes it appealing, practical and possible."

~JUDITH SHERVEN, PhD AND JIM SNIECHOWSKI, PhD
Best-selling authors of *Be Loved for Who You Really Are*

"*The Freedom Formula* reveals a massively important message.... that bringing your spiritual beliefs into business is the only true path to success. This book provides an authentic and powerful approach for combining passion and profit."

~ARIELLE FORD
Author of *The Soulmate Secret*

"If you are interested in deepening the soul of your business and relationship to Divine Order in any work environment, this upbeat and enlightening book will show you where to begin. Christine's practical action exercises will jump-start your journey toward conscious business success. Read it and feel empowered!"

~Charlene M. Proctor, Ph.D.
Best-selling author of *Let Your Goddess Grow!*
and *The Women's Book of Empowerment*

"Finally—someone who brings consciousness and awareness to the business of making money. Christine Kloser takes us on a thrilling adventure of what business could be like if it had both heart and mind. The result is a guidebook on how to transform yourself, your clients, your business and the world."

~James Roche
Business and Marketing Strategist

THE
FREEDOM
FORMULA®

How to Put *Soul* in Your Business…
and *Money* in Your Bank

CHRISTINE KLOSER

Capucia LLC
York, PA

Published by:
Capucia, LLC
211 Pauline Drive #513
York, PA 17402
www.capuciapublishing.com

ISBN: 978-1-945252-51-8
Library of Congress Control Number: 2018959701

Cover Design: CANDesigner
Layout: Aldren Gamalo
Editor and Proofreader: Corrine Dixon
Author photos: Ken Rochon and Monika Broz

Printed in the United States of America

To the dreamers, misfits
visionaries, catalysts, and
leaders who believe a
better world for all is
within our reach.

Let Your Business Lead You

Let your business lead you.
Let it guide you
to those places in your heart you have yet to discover.
Let it call your Soul
to be fully expressed and engaged in the world.
Let it be the way
for you to contribute your unique gifts and serve others.
Let it be your tool
for making the planet a better place.
Let it be your vehicle
for leaving a legacy long after you are gone.
Let it be YOU…
…mind and body, heart and Soul.
~Christine Kloser

CONTENTS

CHAPTER 4

Implement Your New Business Vision   117

CHAPTER 5

Maintain Your Energy and Realize Your Dreams 139

FOREWORD

Is it possible, even feasible, to incorporate spirituality into your business and still be able to build a highly successful enterprise? Most definitely yes!

Some people would laugh at such a concept, but I've been saying for quite some time that business, and the way you do business, is your Highest spiritual understanding demonstrated.

It is in business and commerce where the world will turn toward a new idea about itself because nothing turns the wheels of life faster, or more consistently, than business and commerce. Ever it has been and ever it will be, since the way we interact with each other, the way we transact the business of life, is crucial to the experience of the creation of life itself.

I want to emphasize that there is no such thing as a separation between business and spirituality. It's time to stop disintegrating yourself, because in so doing you disintegrate life itself. To understand this key principle and the important process of recreating ourselves anew is to understand it begins with the recreation of the way you do business, the way you undertake commerce. So, this is a vitally important topic for you to understand because… business IS your Highest spiritual understanding demonstrated.

In this book, Christine Kloser beautifully explains how to integrate your spiritual nature with proven business principles to become a successful, conscious entrepreneur. Christine's unshakable belief in operating her businesses according to her Highest spiritual understanding has led to the creation of this straightforward spiritual approach to business… for the purpose of having YOUR highest spiritual understanding demonstrated, and positively impacting the world through your business.

If you've been searching for a way to enrich your business by adding the spiritual essence of who you are, trusting in your Divine Plan, and cementing your connection to your Source AND your clients, then keep reading.

You'll enjoy the journey!

~NEALE DONALD WALSCH

P R E F A C E

T hank you for allowing this book to come into your life at this exact moment in time. As with everything you've ever experienced, this book being in your hands right now is part of your Divine Plan.

After reading the prior paragraph, either you'll think I'm crazy for speaking of your Divine Plan in the context of a "business" book, or you'll be captured by my words because they resonate with your Soul. If the latter is true, you've probably been looking for confirmation that the desire to blend your business aspirations with your spiritual beliefs and principles IS the right way for you to BE in business.

You can take a refreshing and relaxing deep breath now. You have found your home in this book. You're not alone in your desires to integrate these two worlds (Spirit and business); in fact, you are part of a growing number of conscious entrepreneurs who view their business as the perfect vehicle for their Highest Self-expression in the world, their freedom.

Throughout the book, sometimes I'll refer to God, and when I do I'm not pointing to any particular religion. I'm referring to the Universal Source of unseen energy that exists in and around every living thing; the Source that causes and sustains life in all shapes and forms. I personally refer to this energy as God. But, if the word God doesn't resonate with you, replace it with whatever word feels like a fit for you. The important matter is for you to get the information in this book, because you attracted it to yourself for a reason. So, if that means replacing the word God with Energy, Spirit, All That Is, Source, or anything else, that's OK with me. Do what works for you!

My intention in your reading this book is that it'll have a transformative effect on your Self, your clients and customers, your family, your friends, your health, your Spirit, your relationship with God… everything. For, God truly is your ultimate business partner and the Source through which all things come to you. It's time to bring that energy more presently and more fully into your life… and your business. After all, there is no separation between your spirituality, your business and your life; it is all ONE. We are all one.

To your freedom!

Christine

INTRODUCTION

~~~~~

Thank you for picking up this book and reading it! One thing I know about you already is you're a business owner/entrepreneur (or want to be). The other thing I know about you is that you place FREEDOM very high on your priority list. In fact, you'd likely give up security and stability for the freedom to pursue your dreams, live the life you feel destined for and experience the Highest expression of yourself in your business and your life.

In addition to wanting freedom, you are also a spiritual being. Your spiritual beliefs and understandings form a strong foundation for your life. And, while you may not meditate or pray every day, you believe in a power much greater than yourself. No matter where you go, or what you encounter, you trust there is an Order to everything; and everything you experience falls under that Order one way or another, including your business.

It's easy to find books about business, and books about spirituality, but it is hard to find books that outrightly combine both topics under one cover. I personally needed a 'manual' for how to bring spirituality into my business—not just my life—on an ongoing basis. When I couldn't find this manual anywhere, I set out to create one and thus *The Freedom Formula*® was born.

My basis for *The Freedom Formula* was probably created the moment I hopped in a 1987 Volkswagen Fox with two girlfriends after I graduated college. I was moving 3,000 miles away from my home in Connecticut to pursue a new life in San Diego, California. Although I wasn't aware of it at the time, my quest for freedom had begun. I felt called to create a new, fulfilling, exciting and purposeful life. So, I went as far away from that old 'normal' life as I could… without having to leave the continental United States. Thankfully, my life defies any picture of normal; rather, I've designed it to work for me. And that's what *The Freedom Formula* is about… a life (and a business) that work for YOU spiritually, financially and emotionally!

The Freedom Formula is the culmination of 27 years of entrepreneurial experience, ongoing personal development, continual spiritual evolution and my insatiable curiosity (fellow Sagittarians will relate to that). I have been bringing together the concepts in this new edition for nearly 30 years, with some of my greatest discovering in the decade after the first edition was published in 2008. So much has changed since that time, and yet the core remains the same… *The Freedom Formula* hasn't changed at all. It looks like this:

$$(S + C + D + I) \times E = F$$

and stands for this:

$$(Soul + Connection + Design + Implementation) \times Energy = Freedom$$

Don't worry. It'll make a lot more sense by the time you finish this book.

My quest to achieve personal freedom and spiritual expression, combined with having an intense curiosity, led me to interview or host seminars and events for more than 175 thought-leading experts on the topics of business and or spirituality. I wanted to learn everything I could from well-established, conscious and very successful authors and entrepreneurs: not only for myself, but to share their wisdom with you as well. Some of the experts I've interviewed include:

- Neale Donald Walsh, author, the *Conversations with God* series
- Michael Gerber, author, *The E-Myth*
- Martha Beck, author, and columnist for *O, the Oprah Magazine*
- Seth Godin, author, *The Dip*
- Marianne Williamson, author, *A Return to Love*
- Gary Goldstein, producer of *Pretty Woman*

- Dr. Joe Vitale, author, *The Attractor Factor* and featured in *The Secret*
- Jonathan Fields, author, *How to Live a Good Life*
- Michael Port, author, *Book Yourself Solid*
- Marcia Wieder, author, *Make Your Dreams Come True*
- Loral Langemeier, author, *The Millionaire Maker* and featured in *The Secret*
- Joe Nunziata, author, *Spiritual Selling*
- Susan Piver, author, *The Hard Questions*

Each interview I hosted and each event I produced helped me take the next step along my journey. Each one helped me discover more of who I am; each one put me on the path that lead to writing this updated book. Here, in these pages, I've brought together what I've learned, discovered and created for myself, my clients, my business, and the world... so that you, too, can experience freedom in your life.

And, since growth and learning are always happening, I felt an update of this book was due. In this second edition, I've added new content based on what I've come to know over the years since the original publication, as well as insights from my readers. I trust what I've added will deepen the experience you're about to have.

But, before you dive into this book, I'd like you to take a few moments right now to connect with what the word "freedom" means to you. It's a word whose meaning is different to different people. For the purposes of this book, the only meaning that matters is yours.

This book isn't just a book to read. It is meant to be explored, studied, experienced, shared and used as a tool that furthers you on your journey of conscious business success. To get the full impact of the transformation that lies ahead for you in the following pages, engage yourself fully by downloading the action guide at the link below and doing all the exercises.

Better yet, find a book buddy to read (and do) the book with you. I promise, the journey will be worth it. Together, you'll hold each other accountable to complete the book and action guide exercises while supporting each other to implement *The Freedom Formula* into your business and your life.

I've developed the action guide so you have one place to gather your thoughts and ideas as you move through the information in this book and further along your Divine path.

Download and print your action guide now by going to **www.TheFreedomFormula.com/guide**

ACTION GUIDE EXERCISE #1:

Write your definition of freedom as it
pertains to your business.

Action Guide, page 3
www.thefreedomformula.com/guide

Doing the exercise and taking this first step on your
Freedom Formula journey is where you begin to lay the
foundation of your conscious business. Everything else
builds from here.

It's exciting to think about the foundation you are
going to set and the path that lies ahead for you when you
implement *The Freedom Formula* in your life and business. You
are here to do great things and experience your Highest
expression in the world while being of tremendous service
to others.

It doesn't matter where you're from, how old you are,
how long you've been in business, the work you've done in
the past, the struggles you've faced, or the victories you've
won. What matters is that you're here and ready for this
next phase of creating your freedom-based life.

So, even if the clouds above you may appear gray, the
journey you're embarking on is a beautiful and powerful
one. Remember, there is always a blue sky above the clouds,
and a Divine light shining within.

Will You Post A Review on Amazon?
If you like what you read in
The Freedom Formula, I'd greatly appreciate
if you'd post a favorable review on Amazon.
This will help me reach more people
with this message. Thank you!
Go here to post your review:
www.freedomformulareview.com

CHAPTER I

Discover the Soul in Your Business

The Freedom Formula:
$$(\text{Soul} + C + D + I) \times E = F$$

Every business has a Soul: an energy existing inside the business permeating every aspect of the entity and the impact it has on the world. It's the essence of the business: the "thing" that makes your business unique, glorious and a perfect piece in the Divine Order of the Universe. It may be a new concept for you to grasp that your business is a significant element to the Order of the Universe. But, it's true.

Each business exists as an energy, much like each human being exists as an energy; each fulfilling its part in the world. Each part, no matter how small it may seem when viewed as part of the Universe, is significant. This includes you and your business. Here's an example to help you get a feel.

Think about the interior workings of a clock (not a digital one, but one with hands that move). The clock has several gears inside, each one doing its exact job to make sure the clock works. Now, each of those gears has numerous teeth that are necessary to keep the gears going as they're supposed to. If one of those teeth isn't there; the clock won't work. No matter how many other gears and teeth there are, if just one of them is missing the whole system is out of whack.

It's the same way with the Universe, when you consider that every living being is one of those teeth; every one is a piece of an integrated whole. So, if you ever doubt that your business is a significant element to the Divine Order of the Universe, think again. You, your expression in the world and your business are all important pieces of a much greater whole.

I can't claim to fully understand the power of this unseen Universal energy I call God. Perhaps one day when I birth into Spirit, I will have a deeper understanding. But for the purposes of this book, it's important to share that I absolutely believe there is an energy that exists outside of us that has everything to do with everything. It is the ultimate Source of All That Is, and it is always there, no matter what. This energy cannot be turned on or turned off; there is no beginning or end to its supply. It simply IS.

Can I personally prove this is 100% truth? No. But it serves me to BELIEVE it is. Think about it. What is the alternative? To go about your life, and your business, believing it (and you) exists completely separate from everything else? That you are not connected to anything outside of yourself? For me, that would be a horrible existence; to believe there isn't some Higher order to our lives, and that we are not connected by one unified Source. So, I choose to believe. I choose to accept this Energy (God) as true for me. And, I can tell you that once I fully accepted this as true for me and tapped into the unseen energy that is right there in front of, within, and around me… everything changed.

I distinctly remember feeling this shift inside of me and the profound impact it had on every aspect of my life. I used to be one of those people who could never sit still and always had to be doing something. I couldn't even go to the pool with my family without bringing along my computer and a long list of things needing to get done. When I saw other people simply lounging around and looking at the trees, napping or staring at the sky, I couldn't comprehend how they could just sit there and do nothing.

But after going through this shift and feeling a deeper connection to the energy of the Universe I could easily enjoy hours upon hours listening to the birds, watching the clouds change form, feeling the breeze on my face (in other words, doing what I used to consider "nothing"). It was amazing to feel how "nothing" now felt like everything to me. The surprising thing was that the more I rested in this place of connection, the more got done, with more ease and speed than when I was more disconnected and willful in my ways.

That said, your job as an awake, conscious entrepreneur is to allow this energy into your business and your life; to let it flow through you and guide you in your endeavors. As I said earlier, the energy is always there, and can never be "turned off." The only thing that can be "off" is you. If you feel the energy flow is blocked, it is not about the energy, it's about you. This is an important concept for you to grasp. Perhaps not easy, but certainly important. You alone can increase your level of personal responsibility and embrace the fact that you are the creator of your life and can change it, no matter what you're facing.

Somehow, someway, perhaps by simply allowing it to slip from your conscious awareness, you may feel disconnected from that Source... disconnected from the Highest within your Self. This is natural and happens to everyone at different points on the journey. Sometimes the disconnection is caused by stress, anxiety, worry or sometimes because you're just plain tired, burned out and overwhelmed by life. It's okay when this happens. Nobody expects you to be perfect. Yet, it's critical you don't give up and quit.

During these times of disconnection, don't worry. A simple shift in your awareness, or a few deep conscious breaths can bring the feeling of connection back. *The Freedom Formula* is designed to help you maintain that conscious connection and allow it to guide you as you take steps to create the business and life you've always dreamed of. Because when you're living your life connected to Its abundant energy, and consciously connected to the Universal flow of All That Is, your Soul can be fully expressed in the world and you will experience yourself in your glory… as you were born to be.

The Soul of Your Business is…

By now, you may be asking, "then, what exactly IS the Soul of my business?" The answer is simple: the Soul of your business is… you.

As a business owner, your Soul IS the essence of the business. You are the person who birthed the business. You are the person whose creativity brought forth the idea for your company, products and services. You are the person who has a vision and takes steps to realize it. You are the person who believes your business is a vehicle to make a difference in the world, and to be part of the positive evolution of life as you know it. So, you see? The Soul of your business is... you.

But, sometimes after a few months (or years) of being in business, you may lose sight of that initial excitement and connection. Perhaps your business faces some difficult challenges. Maybe you are discouraged that clients didn't flock to you immediately. Perhaps the money you had to start your business has run out. Maybe you're exhausted. All of these situations can arise in business. But, equally, there are things you can do in these times.

One of the most important things you can do first is remember you are not alone in your challenges. Every entrepreneur has peaks and valleys, and moments of doubt. That's part of our experience as business owners, and it's also why so many people would rather suffer in a dead-end job they hate than take the risk to create a life and business they love. The entrepreneurial journey isn't for the faint of heart. Give yourself credit for walking the road less travelled and have compassion for your beautiful self when things aren't going as you'd planned.

Another thing you can do is hop off the treadmill of continuous action and allow the time to reconnect with the spark within you that feels called to create, contribute and cause positive change in the world. *The Freedom Formula* is a journey anchored in the conscious awareness of every aspect of you, your business, the world around you and the abundant energy of the Universe.

ACTION GUIDE EXERCISE #2:

Take a moment to write down the reasons why you started your business.

Action Guide, page 3
www.thefreedomformula.com/guide

To help you with this exercise, here are some things to contemplate. Were you frustrated with a job that drained you? Did other people suggest you do your own thing? Were you inspired by a dream or flash of insight? Did your hobby evolve into something more substantial? Was there simply a deep sense of knowing that you wanted to serve others through your own business? Were you excited about creating your own business culture?

The Four Components of Conscious Business

The key element we're talking about here is increasing your conscious awareness, making it a good time to talk about the elements of being a conscious business owner. These were not on the curriculum when I earned my bachelor's degree in Business Management, and certainly were nothing I learned on a teleseminar or by reading popular business books. The criteria arose from my personal experience and quest to integrate my spiritual nature into my business.

Conscious businesses have four components. I invite you to review these aspects of your business and engage in an honest and purposeful evaluation of where you stand on each of them:

Component #1:
A Conscious Business Makes Money

This was a difficult concept for me to embrace. Like many conscious entrepreneurs, I cared a lot about my customers and clients, sometimes more than I cared about myself. Willing to sacrifice my own needs to help others, I'd give away my time, my knowledge, my ideas, everything… without asking for anything in return. Or I was guilty of significantly underpricing when I did put a price tag on my offerings. I wanted to be of service, and to help as many people as possible. So, I did that at all costs—and it did cost me a bundle—because I didn't want to let anyone down. For that wouldn't be a conscious business, would it? Ha!

Sometimes it's challenging to combine your desire to "serve" with the desire to make money. Is it really possible to combine Mother Teresa and top CEOs? Yes.

I know these two energies feel like they go together as well as oil and water. But, in order to be a successful and profitable conscious business owner you need both. Money is simply a form of energy that is exchanged for the service you provide to the world. You deserve to be well compensated for that!

I believe that in order for our world to survive (and thrive) through these rapidly changing times, it needs you, the conscious entrepreneur, to make a lot of money so you can spread more of your wisdom, love, knowledge, heart and Soul out into the world... giving back in a BIG way!

If you looked up the definition of "business" in Webster's dictionary, you'd see something that says business is "a profit-seeking endeavor." If you do not seek, and realize, a profit, it is not a business. It is a short-lived charity, it is a sinking ship, it's something you'll begin to resent and dread because the lack of money drains every ounce of energy from your being. Elevating to the higher energetic vibrations of Source energy when you don't have enough money for the mortgage is a great challenge. I know because I've been there.

I had built a business on my desire to connect with and be of service to like-minded women entrepreneurs. Money never entered into the equation until I found myself knee-deep in owning a full-fledged women's networking organization. While it appeared to be successful on the outside, I knew the truth. The business wasn't even breaking even. I had to support the business with my own personal savings and credit.

From what members told me, my networking organization was one of the most powerful groups they'd ever experienced. It brought spirituality and business together in the same space (back in 2000 when it was a groundbreaking concept). I loved and cared about the members, and I know they loved and cared about me, too. All of my events for this organization were a "love fest." Women would leave the monthly meetings feeling deeply connected to each other, to themselves, to Source and to their vision for their business. Oftentimes, the hotel banquet manager (where we met) had to kick us out of the banquet room at 11:30 at night, nearly two hours after the meeting had ended! Nobody wanted to leave, especially me! I wanted to drink in every ounce of energy from that conference room.

So, you can imagine the gut-wrenching decision I had to make to shut down the organization. Why? The more I explored the concepts of conscious business, the more I realized my networking organization was an UNconscious business at that time. Because when it came to the financials, I had been operating with blinders on... I was scared to face the truth. How could I run a financially failing business while taking a stand that making money was a core component of a conscious business? I couldn't.

So, I took my own advice and shut down the business. It was one of the hardest things I've ever had to do. It helped that I gave "departing" gifts to each and every member of the organization with a value that far exceeded what they had paid for their membership. Clearing my conscience helped ease my personal sadness and fear of letting down the members.

Making the choice to use my profit-and-loss statement as a guide to determine the close of that business (when my heart told me otherwise) said to the Universe that I was serious about making money. This action in the physical world, along with my willingness to do something that was extremely uncomfortable for me, was a very clear signal something had shifted within: I was ready and felt worthy of receiving a lot more money.

I continued to grow on this edge for another decade, repeating the same pattern in 2011, the year I made another difficult decision to let go of another business, this time losing my home and filing for bankruptcy in the process. However, this time, I did things differently in the aftermath, and by 2015 had grown my new business, serving transformational authors and leaders, to more than $1 million in revenue.

Let me be clear: I'm not asking you to shut down your business. I am asking you to increase your awareness of the financial health of your entity. One of the best ways to do so is to spend some time reviewing your profit and loss statement. Look at the numbers to see if what you're doing is really working in terms of money. When you love your business, and your clients, it can be very challenging to look at your business in a "black and white" way. It sure was (and still is) for me. But, it is necessary. Let's be clear: a business that doesn't make money, isn't a business at all… it's a hobby. This book isn't about hobbies; it's about putting Soul in your business and money in your bank.

Speaking of money, let's quickly clarify something else: while you are meant to attract a lot of it, it's not for the purpose of acquiring material possessions and being able to keep up with the Joneses. Rather, the purpose of the abundance you're meant to receive is to support you to keep up with your Soul's desire to be fully-expressed in the world (more on that later). Trust me, the plan is not for you to be in survival mode for the rest of your life. Money is a means to give you options. It's there to support your life, not be your life.

So, whether you make $50,000, $500,000 or $5,000,000 per year or more, now is a good time to look at the bottom-line of your business.

ACTION GUIDE EXERCISE #3:

It's time to look at your business profit and loss statement to review your gross revenues, income, expenses, debts, and profit to see if your business is trying to tell you something.

Action Guide, page 4

You may want to put on some relaxing music, light a candle and make yourself a cup of tea while you look at the numbers of your business to see and hear what they are saying. Or if candles and tea aren't your thing, do whatever works for you to dig into the numbers. They'll actually speak to your Soul. They'll guide you towards making decisions, decisions that'll help you make more money, be more fulfilled, and experience more joy in your business.

As you reflect on the numbers in your business, please remember to be kind to yourself. If you're facing challenges in this area, "beating yourself up" isn't going to help. Give yourself credit for being willing to look at the finances, which can feel like the least romantic part of your dream. Allow yourself instead to see what you need to see about the financials and use your new understanding to help you grow and shift. You may discover you need to let something go or put more energy into an income stream that is positioned for growth.

The last time I went through this step for my own business, I discovered I had significantly increased my revenues, but I also discovered that some of my highest grossing income streams were also the ones where I felt the highest emotional and personal cost. So, in looking at the numbers, I allowed myself to release some things that weren't working for me personally, and turn my focus towards developing some new offerings that were more aligned with my values and priorities as a working mother and wife.

It's not as much about more money as it is about more LIFE... for you! Looking at the numbers will help you see where things are contracting and where they're expanding. Let the numbers guide you to make conscious choices in your business moving forward from here.

Component #2:
A Conscious Business Makes a Difference

The second component of a conscious business is to make a positive difference in the lives of others. A company producing and marketing a diet pill known to cause damage to the human body is not a conscious business. But the consultant whose deepest commitment is to transform clients' lives, and quite possibly the world, by their sharing of knowledge and wisdom is a conscious business owner.

Thankfully, there are many thousands of businesses that already operate under this context of conscious business. I'm sure you have experienced a few yourself aside from your own business.

For instance, if you have a carpet cleaning business it might not seem like it's making as much of a difference as an alternative health practitioner who restores her patients back to health. Going beyond the obvious, we see that carpet cleaning *does* make a difference in the lives of the people who are having their carpets cleaned. It's helping them live the kind of lifestyle they want to live. It's keeping a cleaner environment for their family. It's supporting the maintenance of a home where the owners are eager to open up their doors and invite friends and loved ones to enjoy space and time in their home.

Under closer examination, a carpet cleaner truly is making a difference to their customers and clients. This value should be the top of mind aspect when working with a new customer or talking to clients. It's truly connecting with the concept of how you can be of service to them, and how you can positively impact their lives. When you're operating as a conscious business owner, it's not about closing a deal; it's about being of service and opening up a new possibility for your customers and clients.

Occasionally this will mean you'll refer your prospect or client to somebody else, if that referral can better match their needs. The genuine desire to make a difference by serving your prospect or client as best as you possibly can may mean you are not the best one to help them. This can be a difficult concept to swallow. Let me give you an example to illustrate how this works.

Several years ago, I was talking with a potential joint venture partner. We'd been going back and forth for months on this deal that we'd been trying to put together. At one point he asked me something about one of my "competitors." (I put "competitors" in quotes because I don't believe in the concept when talking about it in the context of a conscious business... more about that in component #3.) Rather than panicking I said, "I really appreciate that you asked me about this and here's how our services are different." Make note that I didn't say mine were better, just different.

After explaining the differences in a matter-of-fact way I said, "But I understand as a business person, if you do your research with them and find that they're a better fit for you, it's perfectly okay with me. I want you to work with the person that you are meant to work with, the person with whom you are divinely meant to do this project with. If it's me, fantastic; I am grateful to move forward with you. If it's someone else, then I've really enjoyed getting to know more about you and working with you on the possibility of this project. I'll wish you well. If ever down the road my services might come in handy again, please let me know. I'm here to help."

It felt like a personal "win" to say this and really mean it. At the time, it was probably the biggest deal I had ever worked on, and I was completely detached from the outcome. I trusted that whatever unfolded for both of us would be for our Highest and best good.

This concept is what I'm referring to as the second component of making a difference. It's when you are committed to making such a difference that if your or your prospect's Highest good is going to be best served by not doing business together, you wish them well in working with a different company. In this light, you are truly being of service... to you, them, and the Divine Plan. The space that opens up for new possibilities will surprise you by bringing you more of what you desire, and more of the right clients for you. The saying is true: when one door closes, another door opens.

However, it can be a very scary place to enter, especially when you feel like you "need the money." It is much easier to do when you believe 100% in yourself and your product or service, and you don't have any doubt about what you can (and cannot) provide your clients. The increased confidence you get from having clarity about your products and services, and believing in their value, is a necessary piece of being willing to go to these places to make a difference.

The other piece to contemplate as you considering making a difference through your business is the fact that you making a difference is powerful fuel to help you keep growing and evolving in your business.

If you're like me, you have "off" days now and then (yes, I have them too). And, perhaps the last thing you feel like doing is getting on the phone with a client. However, when you're able to connect at a deep level to the difference you make it will help you rediscover your passion for the work you do.

Recently, I was scheduled to be a guest on a call at night. I rarely say yes to being interviewed at night, but I really wanted to support the people putting on this event. But, I was having one of those "off days" and I was struggling to remember my own brilliance.

So, in order to shift my energy and deliver my best to everyone on the call, I took some time prior to the interview to watch a bunch of client testimonial videos. In the videos, I watched as they thanked me for making such a big difference to them; that after working with me as their coach they opened the floodgates for miracle after miracle to show up for them... in their businesses, for the transformational books they finally wrote, and their lives.

Watching these videos allowed me to reconnect with the difference that I make, and they inspired me so much I gave one of my best interviews ever.

I encourage you to keep a file (on your computer or in your file drawer) of the letters, cards, emails, and videos you receive from clients and customers who share with you how much of a difference you make. Then, remember to pull out this file when you need to reconnect with your brilliance, so you can serve at an ever higher level.

ACTION GUIDE EXERCISE #4:

What is the difference you make in the lives of your clients and customers? How are you positively impacting their lives?

Action Guide, page 5
www.thefreedomformula.com/guide

These are the questions to ask yourself to remain connected to your unique contributions in the lives of others. Maintaining your connection to the difference you're making will get you through the challenges you face along the way.

Component #3:
A Conscious Business Calls You to Be Fully Who You Are

If you've ever felt like you had to hide a piece of yourself in your business, it's not a conscious business. Rather, a conscious business draws forth every ounce of your spirit and calls you to be more of who you are. Your conscious business needs you to be who you are because that is exactly where your success lies.

Too often, business owners feel like they "should" be a certain way in business, and a different way in life. It's just not true. The only way to succeed as a conscious business owner is to be ALL of you, all the time. The very qualities and characteristics that make you, you, are the exact qualities and characteristics your business (and customers and clients) need and want you to be.

It's incredibly challenging to put on your "game face" while trying to fit into someone else's idea of who you should be. Or, worse yet, your own misguided idea of who YOU think you should be. The joy truly comes in surrendering to exactly who you are…. yes, every tender loving ounce of your being: quirks, idiosyncrasies, vulnerabilities and all. Those are the very things that make you who you are, who God meant for you to be the moment you were born.

One side benefit of being fully who you are in your conscious business is that you have no "competition." Nobody can be you. Nobody can duplicate your heart and Soul. Nobody can exude you, but you. So, as you discover and express more of your essence, the more you distinguish yourself in an overcrowded market of entrepreneurs who are trying to be someone else. In so doing, you will become a natural magnet for your best clients, only attracting those customers and clients who are meant to work with you.

As we discussed in the second component, sometimes you may need to turn something (or someone) away from your business if you're not a good fit. So how do you know if it's not the right fit for you? The answer is simple. If you feel yourself being compromised by what or who you're pursuing, or you feel your dream of freedom becoming further out of reach, it's not the right fit. You'll know when this is happening because you won't feel called to be more of who you are. You'll begin to feel contracted, tired, overwhelmed, discouraged or disingenuous.

The process of being more of who you are is a continual and never-ending journey. Don't expect that one day you'll "arrive," be everything you're meant to be, and your business will be smooth sailing for decades to come. It doesn't work that way.

I know from experience that what worked for me and my business a few years ago doesn't necessarily work anymore. As I've grown and changed, my business has had to grow and change with me and continues to! Even with the success I've had, there was sometimes a part of me that began to feel contracted and frustrated with some of it.

In order for me be more of who I truly am, I had no choice but to reevaluate things and make the tough decisions to change course, adjust certain projects and programs, and add new services that made my heart sing at a deeper level. Don't get me wrong, some of these components that needed to change still had great value for clients, but they needed to take a different place in my business. It was through this process that I gave myself permission to be more of who I am and experience more joy and freedom in my business.

Being who you are is the strongest asset you can have as a business owner. The "secret formula of you" can never be knocked-off. And, oh, what fun it is to discover that your most important role in your business is to be more of your Divine Self. How lucky you are that this is your Highest mission in your business, and your life. How blessed you are that deep down inside you probably already know this. Perhaps right now you're even nodding your head "yes" in thankful agreement that you get to discover and share more of yourself through your business. Awesome, isn't it?

So, I invite you to BE the glorious person you are. Embrace everything that feels easy, natural and graceful. These very things guide you to experience more of yourself. While these experiences that are most natural to you may not seem like anything spectacular, they are, in fact, everything. They don't seem extraordinary to you because of how innate they are to who you are. Success is supposed to be easy. When you're simply being yourself and doing all that comes naturally as your Divine Self, success flows.

Action Guide Exercise #5:

~~~

Identify your natural gifts.

Action Guide, page 6
www.thefreedomformula.com/guide

Component #4:
A Conscious Business Trusts In Its Divine Plan

The fourth component of conscious business success is to trust in your Divine Plan. This means to always know—no matter the challenge, no matter how much a particular client might be driving you up the wall, no matter how much you're pulled off track—that you continue to step forward in every moment and trust that your Divine Plan is unfolding perfectly in your life. And you do this without panicking when lower vibration emotions (anger, resentment, fear, shame, judgment, etc.) start creeping in.

One of my clients asked, "What do I do when I feel a sense of lack or doubt coming into my mind and my Divine Plan feels nowhere to be seen?" The answer is simple, but not necessarily easy in the moments of distress. And that is to reconnect back to Source energy. When you feel lower vibration emotions rising within you, it's time to make a conscious shift away from the dark, downward spiral of those emotions. You do this by elevating your awareness to the vibration of God/Source, making it easier to realize that the experience you're having is literally a "blip" in relation to the Divine Plan for your life. It is this awakening, this elevation of consciousness, which allows you to see the Divine Plan, so you can surrender to it, and know that all is well.

There is a myriad of ways to reconnect with Source and rediscover trust in your Divine Plan. We'll cover a few of them in the next chapter. One of my favorite methods to shift my vibration and embrace trust in my Divine Plan is to listen to guided meditations. This is a tool I have used, and continue to use, in my life, and I'm convinced that guided meditations were my saving grace when I experienced some huge challenges in the past. So I've made it easy for you to take advantage of this same tool. I've recorded a meditation for you to download immediately at *www.TheFreedomFormula.com/guide.* It's called, "Trust in Your Divine Plan" and it'll gently guide you back to your trusting heart and peace of mind.

Please take some time today to download and listen to this guided meditation.

┌──┐

ACTION GUIDE EXERCISE #6:

~~~⤜⤛~~~

Journal your thoughts on your Divine Plan after listening to the meditation.

Action Guide, page 6-7
www.thefreedomformula.com/guide

└──┘

After you listen to this guided meditation, take a few moments to write down the insights and understanding you received in this process.

Another very helpful tool to bring you back to your center and back into trusting in your Divine Plan is to breathe. Deep, conscious breathing is one of the most powerful and instantaneous tools you have access to anywhere, for free, to shift your state of being in a heartbeat.

When you want to connect with your Higher Self or connect to trusting in how your Divine Plan is unfolding, simply give yourself a few minutes to close your eyes, take several deep breaths and drop your awareness down into your heart. You may want to place your hands over your heart and ask to receive some guidance or a message from your Higher Self. You'll be surprised to see what comes through for you when you allow yourself to slow down and reconnect with the Divine presence within you.

Or perhaps you're someone who likes movement to help you shift your vibration. If that's you, get up and dance, go for a walk, hit the gym, jump on a trampoline, hula hoop, vacuum your house or do some yard work. Just don't sit there and do nothing. When you know you need a "state change," get up and move your body in a way that feels right for you. Sometimes the simple act of standing up can make a difference!

How Are You Doing?

Now that you know the four components of conscious business success:

1) Make money; 2) Make a difference; 3) Be fully who you are; and 4) Trust in your Divine Plan, it's time for you to do a self-assessment.

Take a moment right now to honestly assess how you're doing in each of these four criteria (I is not doing well and 5 is doing great):

1. My business makes money	I	2	3	4	5
2. My business makes a difference	I	2	3	4	5
3. My business calls me to be more of who I am	I	2	3	4	5
4. I trust in my Divine Plan	I	2	3	4	5

There are no right or wrong answers. Please, do not use this assessment as a tool to judge yourself. It is meant only to be a vehicle for elevating your awareness (becoming more conscious) of where you stand in this moment of time, as it pertains to you and your conscious business.

If you didn't score high on every criterion, but wish you could, that's OK. Just having this realization means you are much further on the path than you were before you cracked open the cover of this book. Now you know the areas that need your focus, intention and attention.

What Were You Thinking?

We can't address the concepts of consciousness and awakening without also exploring the influence your thoughts have on your reality, because every thought, intention, idea, image, feeling, experience, success, failure, opportunity and challenge have brought you to where you are in your life right now. Of this entire list, however, your thoughts and intentions are the most powerful. When you begin to fully comprehend that your thoughts and intentions create your reality, you'll see that where you stand today is a culmination of all of your past thoughts.

Don't like what you see from where you stand right now? Your present stand is a result of the thoughts that have persisted in your past. And that's good news! Why? Because the more aware you become of the power of your thoughts, the easier it becomes to work on shifting them to create a different future.

Everything that's occurred in your past to cause every thought you've had... has divinely directed you to now. And, now is such a beautiful gift because it is where all future creation begins.

Take a moment to reflect on this concept. I'm serious. Right now take at least three deep breaths and connect with all that's occurred to bring you right here right now, and the understanding that it has been divinely directed. Let a sense of peace settle into your bones as you breathe and reflect on this. Honor your journey. Celebrate who you've become. Acknowledge the struggles you've overcome. Allow yourself to feel the power of this moment. Right now is where your future begins.

While we're talking about the beginning, let's go back to your beginning in this life. When you were born you were closely connected to the Divine; you were born as a radiant being, filled with light, love, grace, acceptance, and a deep connection to the Spirit that brought life forth through you. At the moment of your birth, there was no fear, doubt, scarcity, lack, or wondering if you were enough. You just were. And, you were more than enough. You knew with your first breath you would always be OK because the Source that created you would always be there.

But, along the way, you forgot what you knew then. You learned from others who lost sight of the Divinity within them. You were told what was right and wrong, told what to believe and not believe. Maybe you were taught to believe that money was the root of all evil, that you should be seen but not heard, that you shouldn't believe in "pipe dreams," that you had to work hard to make money, and that financial success was the only measure of a person. It's unfortunate these thoughts were projected on you, most likely both consciously and unconsciously. Or maybe the way you interpreted certain experiences impacted you deeply. The good news is now you get to think your own thoughts and eliminate the old thoughts that no longer serve you. You are at the helm of the wheel of your own life; you are the captain who steers your own thoughts. So, it's time to reframe some of your old programming.

For instance, money isn't the root of all evil, it's the source of good in the world (when it's in the right hands); your voice should be heard loud and clear and never squelched; in God's eyes you were born to fulfill your "pipe dreams" (after all they were given to you by Source); money comes to you not through laborious work but the inner work of being fully who you are in the world. You are not measured by the amount of money you make or things you acquire, but by the joy you experience and spread in the world.

I realize there are people who do measure worth by how much money one has in the bank, the car they drive or the position they hold in society. But even if you have people like that in your life, stand firm in knowing that your worth is so much more than money. And, that it's totally okay to also want to attract a lot of it!

Just in case there's a single cell in your being that's thinking, "It's not spiritual to be rich..." listen up one more time! You absolutely, without a doubt, were born to experience abundance in all forms. The only way to be fully expressed as a conscious entrepreneur (not a hobbyist) is to have the freedom to engage in the experiences that allow you to discover more of yourself, and to express yourself through your growing business. And, some of those experiences require money!

Conscious entrepreneurship is about making a positive, lasting impact on the world... through your business. You have a message to share, valuable information that can change people's lives and you want to reach the 'masses.' The reality about fulfilling this vision and dream is that it takes money to grow and sustain your business at this level of success. You need systems, structures, marketing and a support team in place to help you do all this. So, money is a necessity in order for your business to make its greatest contribution. Certainly, if you have the desire for a profitable, expansive conscious business... you also have the ability to manifest everything you need to realize this dream. Yet, keep in mind, one thing money cannot buy is happiness. Happiness is a state of mind you can experience anytime, anywhere... if you are truly present on your journey.

That being said, however, money *can* buy you leverage. It makes it possible to hire the right people to handle the tasks you don't enjoy doing; you're freed up to do what you love. Money allows you to buy more education and travel to meet colleagues and teachers who can help you grow and expand as an individual, and a business owner. Money makes it possible to put systems and structures in place that make your business run even when you're not there. Money buys leverage, and leverage gives you more freedom.

Let me just pause to say that there are amazing people who have done, and are doing, incredibly valuable work in the world and making a massive impact without being materially wealthy (just think of Mother Teresa). She was probably one of the wealthiest people in terms of freedom—she did what she wanted, when she wanted, with whom she wanted, while always having her needs met financially and making a huge difference in the world.

Here, we are talking about conscious entrepreneurship. That is the context in which I emphasize the importance of you receiving and leveraging money and resources to help you achieve your dreams.

OK, so we've gotten clear about what constitutes a conscious business. And I trust since you're reading this right now that you're on board with this way of doing business. So, let's explore a bit more about this first step in *The Freedom Formula*: discovering the Soul of your business.

Your Multi-Faceted Life

Seeing that the Soul of your business is YOU, you can't proceed any further without taking a look at every facet of your life right now. You see, your business is only one facet of your life, although sometimes it feels like everything. The truth is your business reflects EVERY area of your life.

That being said, it's time for you to take an inventory of your life. The interesting thing about this inventory is that all of these areas are integrated into the one (and only) life you will live in this physical body. So, you're not looking at these areas to identify points of separation, you are looking at them to seek threads, themes, consistencies, unity, and ultimately, a fully integrated picture of your life.

Following is a list of the areas of your life you'll be assessing. For each of these areas, when asked, please answer these questions:

1. What is your current experience in that area?
2. What is your level of emotional satisfaction in that area?
3. What are your challenges in that area?
4. What is your Highest vision in that area?

You'll do a lot of writing during this exercise, which is a good thing. The more clarity you have about where you are now (not just limited to your business), the more power you have in transforming your life and achieving new dreams. Clarity IS power.

ACTION GUIDE EXERCISE #7:

Answer the previous four questions
as a discovery tool for a full, personal,
life assessment, as they pertain to
the following areas of your life.

Action Guide, page 8-15
www.thefreedomformula.com/guide

Your Life Assessment

- Personal (emotional health, physical well-being, relationships, family, passion, purpose, etc.)
- Spiritual (your relationship with the Highest part of your Self)
- Financial (your overall financial health and wealth)
- Business (the vision, operations, staff, system, plan, marketing, delivery, etc.)

What's Working for You?

After you complete the exercise, but before you go another step further, it's important now to clearly identify what is working (and what isn't working) for you. It's time to look at your inventories and note those areas that are going incredibly well, also noting those areas that bring the most dissatisfaction and stress. (There's space in your action guide to write about this, too.)

ACTION GUIDE EXERCISE #8:

Write down what is (and what's not) working for you.

Action Guide, page 16
www.thefreedomformula.com/guide

From here, you can begin to release what isn't working and focus on what IS working so you can be free to live your Highest vision for your life. Something to keep in mind as you reflect on those things that may need to be released is this: if it's not working for you, it's not working for God either. In God's world, you are meant to experience joy, and do that which feels natural and easy. These natural and easy experiences are the ones that bring you more connection to the Divine and closer to the full expression of who you are.

But, let's face it. Joy can be pretty far out of reach when you find yourself continually bogged down taking action on tasks that drive you nuts. Every entrepreneur can relate to this. You can tell by the way you FEEL if, on one hand, you're stuck in dead-end details, or if you're doing something that really "lights you up."

Shorten Your "To Do" List

So, let's figure out what "lights you up" so your emotional state rises to the higher, more positive emotions where creativity, abundance, opportunity and joy are a limitless experience!

The way you'll do this is by bringing a new perspective to your "to do" list by filtering it through a four-step process. This is a great way to discover more about where you are at and begin to put more of your Soul into your business, by eliminating those things that drag you down.

ACTION GUIDE EXERCISE #9:

Answer the questions and follow the steps below.

Action Guide, page 17-21
www.thefreedomformula.com/guide

The Action Guide has a page dedicated to each of these five headings:

1. Current "To Do" List
2. For Someone Else
3. Get Done Later
4. Not Worth Doing
5. "Lights me up" tasks

First, take a few minutes to write down all of those items on your current "To Do" list. Simply bring to mind different aspects of your life (including business, of course) and write a laundry list of everything that you do. This can be an overwhelming task, so take a few deep breaths and know that as you get more clarity about where your time and energy are being spent, you can begin to take control of how you want to purposefully invest your time and energy to achieve your dreams; rather than simply doing what's in front of you because it's there to be done.

Once your list is complete, begin to categorize each task by asking yourself these four questions. Once the answer is clear, write that task on the appropriate page.

1. Can someone else do this task, instead of me? If so, whom?

    -Write these tasks on your "For Someone Else" page.

2. Can this task get done later? Nothing is as urgent as you think.

    -Write these tasks on your "Get Done Later" page.

3. Is this task worth doing at all? Some tasks don't matter in the long run.

    -Write these tasks on your "Not Worth Doing" page.

4. Is this a priority for you? Will it bring you joy, and more money?

    -Write these tasks on your "Lights Me up" Page.

Now, I realize that executing this four-step plan for each and every task may be a stretch for you, especially if you're new in business and don't have someone to delegate to yet. In that case, I suggest you seek out an intern from your local community college, hire someone on www.upwork.com or www.fiverr.com or perhaps a local stay at home mom. Do whatever it takes to get someone on board to handle some of the menial details. Begin to get rid of annoying tasks by delegating the things that drive you most crazy. It's not a good strategy to do things that make you want to pull your hair out!

However, it is a "must do" to make sure you understand the tasks you are delegating and have enough knowledge of the task at hand prior to turning it over to someone else. I learned this lesson the hard way and invested hundreds of thousands of dollars in people I hoped would do what needed to be done. However, without first stretching out of my own comfort zone to learn what I wanted to delegate, I simply couldn't delegate or lead from an empowered place. Bottom line is this... before you turn over a task or project, you must first understand it yourself, so you're empowered rather than disempowered in the delegation process.

Here's something else to keep in mind as you get other people to help you with those things you don't like doing. The people who help you with those tasks love doing them. I know it was difficult for me to comprehend that someone actually liked handling that stuff for me. But, my team would tell you that they love what they do. Here's the beauty in this... not only do YOU get to express more of your Highest Self by doing those things that "light you up," but those people who support you in the pursuit of your dreams get to experience more of their Highest Self, too. It's a win-win situation that just can't be beat.

The ultimate purpose of filtering your tasks through this four-step process is for you to shorten the number of items on YOUR priority "To Do" list. Because once it gets shorter, you have more space to "be;" and your "To Do" list becomes comprised of tasks that bring you joy, tasks that "light you up." So, you experience more of who you are meant to be by doing more of these things that bring you joy. Yes, you get to BE more joy, more love, more fulfillment, more light, more expression, more connection, more peace, more of everything. And, this is the place where everything flows, meaning your dreams can be realized more quickly and easily.

In fact, at the end of one of my 3-Day Transformational Writing Retreats, my clients looked at me and couldn't believe how fired up and joyful I was. I had just spent three days doing a deep dive with a few dozen authors to help them write their transformational books. They thought I "should" be exhausted and tired at the end of the final day... ready for the event to be over. But the work I was doing was on my "Lights Me Up" page and it showed. I could have easily kept going for another three days.

This is the benefit of identifying your "Lights Me Up" list. Since doing this process for myself, I've designed my business so I get to facilitate retreats and seminar at least five times a year. Being in person with people, connecting eye to eye and face to face, is what lights me up... and now I get to do that more than ever before in my business. I simply love this time with clients!

Plus, I balance it with my home life because being with my amazing husband and daughter also lights me up. How that looks is that I facilitate the majority of my events in my hometown in York, PA. Rather than me traveling away from my family, I have clients come to me. I even host client events in my home so they can hang out with my family. In this way, I get to do work that fuels me and serves my clients in a big way, and enjoy the evenings and mornings being a wife and mom.

I used to think it was selfish to design my business in a way that worked for every area of my life, but it's not selfish at all. It allows me to serve more. You see, your client knows when they are being served by someone who is fired up and in their joy. They feel it and it lights them up too.

I even took it so far as to design my business offerings to allow me to travel to exotic beach destinations because I love the beach, especially when it's in places like Costa Rica, Tulum, Bahamas, etc. I host Transformational Writing Retreats in places like this once a year because it lights me up and my clients get a ton of writing done listening to the waves and watching the sunset over the ocean. Doing what lights me up, lights them up too. You see how that works?

Let Go... To Soar

I'd like to issue a mild warning here. Through this process of assessment, evaluation and self-reflection in discovering the Soul of your business, you may find you're someplace you don't want to be. You may be years into a business (or a piece of your business) you don't want to be in. Perhaps you've invested thousands of dollars and hours into a strategy that isn't working.

Do yourself a favor. Take a deep breath right now and trust that all is unfolding in Divine perfect order, even if this is bringing up some lower vibration emotions (like fear) about what to do. If this is your current experience, please understand that this, too, is part of your Divine journey; that the very experience of discontent or confusion is an essential piece to get to clarity and joy. Trust me when I tell you that I am only in this joyful place in my business now because of severe discontent and confusion, and hard decisions. These things can actually serve you if you're open to learning from them.

So, if you find yourself (like I did) knee-deep in something that isn't working, you have one of two choices to make: quit or keep going. Seth Godin's succinct book *The Dip* talks about this concept beautifully. Sometimes it makes sense to quit and sometimes it's worth sticking out what Seth calls "the dip."

It's important at this point to also discuss sunk costs. Those are expenses you've paid out in your business that you will never recover. Sunk costs are part of nearly every business—especially those committed to growth—so don't let that be a reason to quit when you really ought to keep going.

You'll need to spend some time assessing your particular situation to determine if you want to forge forward or not. If you choose to let something go, it's imperative that you don't attach yourself to it as a failure. Every "failure" is simply a new understanding, a new insight, a new wisdom, a step to a new and better endeavor.

I shared earlier about the pain I went through in letting go of my business and going through bankruptcy and foreclosure, but, let me tell you, the experience I gained, and who I became as a result of that experience, is one of the most critical pieces to where I stand today. My current business could never have grown like it has if I had held on to the dead weight of a financially unsound and emotionally draining business endeavor. Please keep this in mind if you're going through a release in your business. You're not alone; it's been done before and if it's truly the right thing to do, you'll be amazed at what transpires through your act of courage in letting go.

It's time to give up any lingering conversation about having to struggle or pay your dues. It's an irrelevant concept. Your job is to feel good and vibrationally (energetically) matched to that which you want and desire.

The Spiritual Practice of Leap Frog

We can't talk about being a vibrational match without talking about the concept of leapfrogging. This is a concept that eliminates the old corporate paradigm of ladder climbing; the concept of having to "pay dues" or "work hard and struggle" to get ahead.

Leapfrogging, in my opinion, is a spiritual practice. It's about being in a state of vibration that is in resonance with that which you say you want. For instance, if you're a $75/hour coach and feel comfortable with that rate, you would leapfrog by doing the inner work to have your vibration shift into alignment with being a $250/hour coach, if that's what you desire.

There isn't any law that says you have to work hard or climb ladders to get ahead. The Universe says, 'even before you ask I will have answered.' So, what you're asking for is already there for you, and you'll see it when your thoughts, emotions and energy are aligned with your Highest intentions. What I mean by that is, if you say you want to be a $250/hour coach and feel like a fake when you say it, then, of course, the Universe cannot deliver on such a misaligned intention.

So, your real job in "leapfrogging" is doing the inner work of having your thoughts and emotions fully resonate with what you say you want. This, my friend, is the awakened path of the conscious entrepreneur. It's a continual evolution in your awareness, your expression, your thoughts, your intentions and your connection to the unlimited Source that provides you everything you desire. In truth, it is already there waiting for you to claim it.

I'll share a quick story about my personal experience in learning to "leapfrog." It was after one of my *Transformational Author Experience* trainings where I was stepping back into mentoring clients after a six-year hiatus.

In those six years I had never charged more than $10,000 for any of my programs, even though my colleagues and consultants all said I should be charging at least double. But now I was stepping forward as the *Transformational Author Coach* who pioneered the transformational author movement and had trained more than 70,000 hopeful authors in more than 100 countries. So, as I began the journey of developing my new mentoring program and rate structure, I took into consideration my vast experience, my life, the value of my time, the types of clients I wanted to work with and then created an offering that met all of my needs.

When I crunched the numbers and honestly assessed what my rate should be, I nearly fell over. My calculations showed a figure that was multiples of my previous highest price offering.

I experienced quite a challenge saying the number without coughing or justifying myself as soon as I said the price. So, I spent a lot of time meditating on the number, worked with my own coach, and team, and did a lot of inner work to come up with a fee that felt like a big stretch to me... and also felt like it was high value. I knew I hit the right mark when I sold out my first six mentoring spots in a couple of weeks. I leapfrogged myself into a whole new category and, as a result, attracted clients who also leapfrogged into their deepest work to write their transformational books. It was a win-win for all of us!

I believe that if I had set a fee that didn't feel energetically and emotionally aligned with, I wouldn't have sold out all six spots. The Universe would have known I had thoughts of doubt, fear, unworthiness, etc., which is why this process doesn't work without the spiritual aspect of being in alignment with what you say you want. It only works when it's right for you on every level. Don't worry if it takes you a while to make your first big leap. The good news about leapfrogging is that after you've done it once, it gets easier to leap again and again and again.

Be Here Now

Everything you've learned in this chapter is about getting to the Soul essence of your Self, which IS the Soul of your business. It's about having clarity on where you stand right now. You simply can't get to your destination (your dreams) if you don't know your starting point. A sure-fire way to post-pone your success is to skip this important step of discovery. That is not my wish for you. There's a reason why the first element of *The Freedom Formula* is a mandatory discovery process. Nothing fulfilling or freeing can happen without it.

If you glazed over (or ignored) the exercises in this chapter, now's your time to go back and do them. This is your opportunity to awaken, and to discover what you need, so you can experience true freedom within yourself, and total fulfillment in your business.

CHAPTER 2

Connect to Your Source...
and to Your Market

(Soul+ Connection + D + I) x E = F

Once you've gone through the steps in the previous chapter (to discover the Soul of your business, and gain clarity about where you are), then it's time to make the connections needed for your success. So, the second step of *The Freedom Formula* is to connect, connect, connect.

As you probably noticed, the title of this chapter is about connecting to your Source AND to your market. Only in a book about conscious business can I talk about connecting to your Source and your market in the same sentence. The reason why I've combined these two topics in one chapter is because you need to have both of these connections operating simultaneously if you're going to realize long-term, sustainable success in your business.

The integration of the tangible and intangible, spiritual and practical, visible and invisible parts of your business and your life are the foundation for your conscious business success. Without the integration of these two worlds, there is no Conscious Business.

Many business owners, unfortunately, focus only on one aspect or the other. They're either very focused on their market (and their marketing) or they're focused on their connection to Source and their spiritual evolution. In fact, one of my colleagues admitted she had basically dismissed her spiritual practice for nearly six years in pursuit of her business and marketing goals. After some deep reflection, she realized she needed to embrace both sources of connection in order to experience more success in her business and enjoy a deep sense of purpose and fulfillment in her work. She hesitates to think about what her business could have been today, had she not given up her spiritual path all those years.

Chances are that you lean toward connecting to one aspect more than the other. So, let's identify what your natural tendency is by taking a look at which one of these scenarios resonates most with you. As you read the following scenarios, keep in mind it is not an exercise in judgment, rather one to become more aware.

Please pick the scenario that most resonates with how you live your life now:

Scenario 1: You are busy from the moment you wake up to the time you go to sleep. You check email and/or social media a dozen times a day and find yourself consistently feeling that you have to "do more." You're excited about the prospects of marketing your business and getting more customers... and earning more money. You haven't meditated, journaled or enjoyed any spiritual connection on a regular, daily basis and you keep wondering when it's going to get easier, and when you'll have more time for yourself.

Scenario 2: You are deeply enmeshed in your spiritual journey, and sometimes it consumes you. You don't feel particularly motivated to take practical action in your business, and procrastination feels like your middle name. You feel very connected to your Source/God and would rather spend time on your spiritual pursuits than implementing a marketing plan.

Once you've identified which scenario is most like you, you'll clearly see if you lean more toward your spiritual nature or your practical/business nature.

Conscious business requires both aspects of your business. It requires you to be conscious and grounded in your Higher Self and the creative energy of the Universe.

It also requires you to pay attention to the "business of business" on the physical, tangible plane. So, if you're serious about being on this journey, which I trust you are if you're reading these words, you'll find it worth your while to bring more balance into embracing both energies outlined above: the "take action in the physical world" energy AND the "spiritual evolution" energy.

Understand that doing this will require you to stretch out of your comfort zone. If math isn't your thing, there may be a period of discomfort in looking at the numbers, learning about them and discovering how they can help you make empowered decisions for your business. It's the same idea, if connecting to your Highest Self, God, or the Universe isn't yet part of your everyday life, where you may be somewhat uncomfortable to begin to spend time meditating, journaling, praying or simply connecting to that Source on a daily basis. Embrace the discomfort and know that it'll be well worth it in the long run.

The reason you need to embrace BOTH aspects in your business is because no matter how connected you are to Source, no matter how much you meditate, pray, visualize and intend... if your goals and dreams are not connected to the *physical world* and the market you serve here on planet Earth then there is no vehicle for your gifts to be received, and, vice versa. If you're consumed by the concrete tangible aspects of your business and your market (and leave your spiritual life at the curb), you're missing out on the most powerful unseen energy in the Universe that is always working in your favor.

Your Divine gifts were given to you for the purpose of sharing them with others, so it's safe to say your gifts are not supposed to remain your best kept secret. And, the fastest way to unlock YOUR secret is to allow yourself to be a conscious conduit of connection to both worlds. *The Freedom Formula* refers to this second step as being connected to Source and to your market.

Your Connection to Source

By this point you may be asking how you can connect more deeply with Source. And, how do you KNOW when you are consciously connected and when you're not? Let me remind you that you are ALWAYS connected to Source, but sometimes you forget. Sometimes your conscious awareness of this connection has completely slipped away. So, how can you stay "awake" and maintain this connection?

Here's where the contemplation of opposites comes in handy to make a point, because it's easy to identify when you aren't connected. You're disconnected when you experience feelings of fear, struggle, doubt, lack, shame, scarcity or anger. It's when life feels hard and you allow yourself to be pulled down by your reality on the physical plane. When you're disconnected it's more difficult to see a light at the end of the tunnel or identify alternate options to solve a problem at hand.

On the other hand, when you are connected to that Source that is outside of yourself it's much easier to manage the experience of the lower vibration emotions such as fear, anger, doubt, etc. because you have a deeper understanding that everything is unfolding for your Highest good, even if it doesn't feel that way in the moment. Those uncomfortable feelings are there for a reason. They serve as guideposts to make you aware that your connection to Source is temporarily turned "off"… and that you have the power to consciously turn the connection back on.

When I was faced with a very challenging financial situation in the past, I spent a lot of time knowing that I was disconnected from Source. I woke up nearly every day feeling panicked about money. How was I going to pay the mortgage? How would I pay my staff? How would I put enough money away for my family's future? Would I need to scrounge up spare change to buy groceries?

I was in a place where I thought it was all up to me to figure out. I was also at a point in my life where I still cared about what other people thought of me, and how embarrassing it would be if anyone knew the truth about my situation. In my mind, nothing could be worse than financial failure.

These old false beliefs kept me in a place of fear, doubt, worry and shame... until I got to a point where the only thing I could do was surrender. Here's what that looked like, how that surrender helped me "turn on" my conscious connection to Source.

However, before I share this story of one of the darkest times in my life, I don't want you to think that times must be dark in order for you to connect with Source energy. For many people, the tough times are the greatest times of growth, but certainly not for all.

I had just finished a conversation with a bankruptcy attorney because I felt that was the only way out of the darkness I was experiencing. I remember sitting on my bed with the phone in my hand, and my husband sitting at the foot of the bed with me. I hung up the phone and cried for a good long while. I couldn't believe it when I heard the attorney say, "It's time to stop paying your credit card bills, and your mortgage." I intellectually knew this was the first step of the gut-wrenching and painful process of filing for bankruptcy and foreclosing on my home, but I just couldn't wrap my head around actually doing that.

All the questions swirled. Where would my family live? Who would ever listen to what I had to say? Could I even get a job if I needed to?

But somewhere in the depths of that emotional storm, I began to sense some ray of hope in the situation. In my moment of despair, I was able to grasp the idea that this, too, was happening for a reason; a Divine reason that would reveal itself to me over time. After all, the only way to go from there was up.

I spent the following few months on my knees, meditating for hours a day. I'd also journal, cry, pray, beg and demand the Universe show me the pony in the pile of manure that my life had become on the outside. All the while, on the inside I felt more peace, hope and joy than I'd ever had before in my life. This is the power of connecting on the Higher, invisible level to the Source of All That Is.

So yes, I did go through with the bankruptcy and lost my home to foreclosure in 2011. Through that experience I become stronger than I'd ever been before. I created rock-solid personal connections to the Source that fueled my every breath as well as to the people I wanted to serve in the world in a new way that felt right in my Soul. And boy oh boy, these connections were powerful and delivered miracles beyond belief into my life.

It was these connections that helped me start anew and create a conscious business that serves transformational authors around the world. The work was so powerful that my business went from $25,000 in revenue in 2011 to over $1 million in 2015.

Please let me say this was the right choice for me. I understand that many people choose to not file bankruptcy and that is the right choice for them. I'm not sharing this story to make a statement about bankruptcy; I share it to make a point about the depth of the moments that can bring about a deeper connection with your Source, your Self and those you want to serve.

And, please remember that not all of these moments of deeper connection come from a negative experience, many times they come from the most joyous experiences of your life.

Maintain Your Connection

So how do you maintain this connection consciously and continually at deeper and deeper levels? That's a good question, and one I trust you'll be on a quest to answer until you leave your earthly body. I believe that one of your Highest purposes in this experience of life on earth is to become closer and closer to that Source and feel the Divine within you. I think it's one of the very reasons why you were born: to remember back to the divinity you knew at your beginning. That being said, I'm going to do my best to share some insights on how to maintain this conscious connection.

Let me first say that on your journey of connecting with Source, there will be moments where you feel it profoundly, and times when you don't feel it at all. This is natural and part of your evolution.

Some moments when you feel it the easiest may be when you hold a new baby in your arms, relax in nature, dance, make love, gaze at the stars or a magnificent sunset, enroll a client you love, listen to music that moves your Soul, experience deep connection with a friend, or look into the joyful eyes of a child. I refer to these as my "woo-hoo" moments. You may have this experience too; when life is so in the flow that you have to holler out loud, "woo-hooooooooo!"

My neighbors probably think I'm a bit crazy, because I'll "woo-hoo" at the top of my lungs with the windows open. You just can't help yourself when the inspired moment hits. In fact, oftentimes when I'm out for a walk in our local park I'll have these moments. I'm in awe at how the air is perfect, the sky is bright blue, and the birds are singing a beautiful song. I find myself walking down the path smiling, and feeling vibrantly alive, saying, "Thank you! Thank you! Thank you!" The moment completely consumes me; I feel deeply connected to Source.

Can you think of moments in your own life when you feel so connected and alive that you just need to let out a "woo-hoo?" I'm sure if you think for a moment you'll discover there are many.

Another way these connection moments express themselves are in what I call "quiet thank you" moments. These are when the deep feeling of God's Presence is nearly beyond words and it's all I can do to close my eyes and whisper, "thank you," often with tears of gratitude welling up in my eyes. I have these moments often when I watch my daughter sleep, am held in the loving arms of my husband, watch a movie like "Wonder," see my rose garden in bloom, or have a client share a tender or vulnerable part of themselves with me... and so many more.

Once you've consciously connected with these "woo-hoo" or "quiet thank you" moments, you'll never forget how they feel. You can always reflect on what it was like to reconnect with that sense of ease, flow, grace, trust, and awe and remember the spark of the Divine within. It's moments like these, and you've had them too, when all is right in the world.

Now, how do you maintain that connection? The answer here is quite simple, but not necessarily easy: you seek to have those experiences more often and with more regularity... including in the simplest or most challenging of moments. As your awareness turns toward these moments of connection and sacredness, you can't help but consciously experience more of them. The key here is continual conscious awareness.

Like this moment, for instance. No matter what your circumstances may be, there is something you can do right now to experience a "woo-hoo" or "quiet thank you" moment. The fact that this book made it into your hands and you're reading this right now is reason enough to be filled with a reflective "thank you." Moments like this are there for you to enjoy, as soon as you focus your attention on noticing them.

Here are a few of my favorite things to do to consciously create "woo-hoo" and "quiet thank you" moments. Let them be reminders of all the possibilities for deep connection in your own life. Maybe you'll even be inspired to enjoy some time right now experiencing one of these: Close your eyes, breathe and remember all you are grateful for

- Read a thank you letter or email from a cherished client
- Call a friend and connect heart to heart
- Prepare a cup of hot tea and write in your journal
- Look for evidence of abundance in your life
- Dance around your living room
- Tell someone you love them
- Take a walk and connect with nature
- Cuddle with your sweetie (or your pet)
- Pray
- Listen to a piece of inspirational music and let it carry your Soul
- Enjoy doing something creative
- Savor a piece of good dark chocolate
- Burn a candle and sit in the presence of its light
- Soak in a warm salt bath
- Play catch with your child (or your neighbor's child)
- Bake cookies and give them away to friends or strangers

Connecting with Source is about your conscious desire (on a moment-by-moment basis) to experience more connection with yourself and with the Divine.

"Woo-hoo" and "quiet thank you" moments are a great place to start. But you'll want to work toward feeling the depth of this connection simply because you are alive and breathing.

Now, I'd like to share another layer of maintaining your connection. It might not sound like fun, but it's a critical piece to make sure you continually experience more conscious connection with Source.

A Disciplined Mind

Discipline. It's not a very warm, fuzzy word. In this context it may even sound a bit harsh because, after all, we're talking about "woo-hoo" and "quiet thank you" moments. But discipline is part of the journey, too.

Have you ever found yourself enjoying a fabulous day where you're in the flow and everything's coming up roses? Then, "something happens" and you are thrown for a loop. Your feeling of well-being is shaken to the core and you need to make a critical choice about how to handle the negativity seeping into your formerly fabulous day. In these situations, you have two choices:

1. Option A: An undisciplined mind would allow whatever happened to pull you straight down to the bottom of the abyss of self-doubt, anger, fear, lack, self-loathing, etc. You pull up a chair and have yourself a big

'ol pity party. After all, you deserve some pity; "something bad" just happened.

2. Option B: A disciplined mind would be fully aware of the power of this moment of choice and would look down the dark abyss and say, "I'm aware that you are calling me into a dark downward spiral, but I consciously choose not to go there." Then, you'll discipline yourself to reconnect to yourself, to the truth of who you are, to your trust in Spirit, and to your belief that the Universe is conspiring for your Highest good... all the time! The disciplined mind takes some action to shift yourself away from the dark abyss of fear.

As you can see, a disciplined mind in this case is not something to resist or ignore. It is the very thing that will help you on a moment by moment basis to rise up and maintain a more joyful and productive state of being.

Another method I want to share with you to help you maintain your conscious connection with Source is something I call a "God's-eye view".

God's-Eye View

Are you familiar with the expression of a "bird's-eye view?" It's when you view things from a bird's perspective, which is far different from what you can see standing on earth. A bird's-eye view allows you to grasp the entire landscape and see the interconnectedness of things that appear separate when you view them from land.

The reason I talk about a "bird's-eye view" is because this concept lead me to facilitate a process at one of my retreats, in which the participants were invited to write about their life from a "God's-eye view." Grasping a sense of your life from that high perspective is an invaluable tool for every conscious entrepreneur to embrace.

What do you think you'd discover about your life right now, where you've been and where you're going? Reflect for a moment and let me say that again. What would the Highest possible perspective say about your life right now, where you've been and where you're going? What dots get connected? What threads do you see woven together? It's an interesting perspective to think about, isn't it?

I doubt that thoughts of lack and limitation would even enter this scenario. Because the singular Universal Source is the ultimate unlimited source of all abundance in the world, and that is exactly the perspective God would have: all things are conspiring for your Highest and most joyous expression in the world. And your good is already there for you.

So, now I invite you into the four-step process of taking a look at your life from this high perspective. Let's get started.

Step 1: Reflect on Your Past

Take a moment to reflect on your past. Identify some of the peaks and valleys of your past experience. Connect with who you've become as a result of all these experiences... the good and the not so good. Look to see how your prior experiences have brought you wisdom, strength, love, insight, commitment, passion, conviction, friendship, resourcefulness, resolve, etc. Allow yourself to see the Divine Order of each and every experience and imagine what God would have said to you at each point along your journey.

Step 2: Connect with This Moment

Next, allow yourself to connect deeply with this moment, and the life that you are currently living. Embrace all of your current success and dreams along with any challenges that may be showing up in your life right now. Allow yourself to fully appreciate the place that you're at today. Again, allow yourself to see the Divine Order of each and every experience. And imagine what God would say to you in this moment.

Step 3: Look to Your Future

Look forward on the path that lies ahead of you. Let your imagination flourish as you envision everything your heart desires becoming real for you. Envision your life as it unfolds in Divine perfection. As you see your future, leave room for things you can't imagine right now... knowing that God's plan for your life is so much bigger than that which you can see from your human perspective. And again, allow yourself to see the Divine Order of each and every future experience and imagine what God would say about the path that lies ahead.

Step 4: Write your God's-Eye View

Now, in a space of quietude, perhaps outside in nature, or in front of a glowing candle, review the above three steps. Begin to write freely about your past, present and future experiences... as if you were God writing about what He sees in (and for) your life. Let your imagination and creativity soar.

ACTION GUIDE EXERCISE #10:

Journal about your God's-Eye View discoveries.

Action Guide, page 22
www.thefreedomformula.com/guide

Take some time with this exercise and write as much as you'd like. The more detail and wisdom you allow to flow through you, the more beneficial this exercise will be for you, especially over time because you'll come back to read this over and over again. Every time you feel stuck, or filled with fear, lack or doubt, you can take out what you've written and remind yourself of the perfection of the Divine unfolding of your life.

The Source of Your Relationships

I didn't want to complete this section on your connection to your Source without bringing to light the value of your relationships in strengthening this connection. You may be asking what your relationships with others have to do with your connection to Source? The answer is everything.

It is through your relationships with others that you're able to experience yourself as an expression of light and love in the world. This holds true in all of your relationships, both business and personal. They are all vehicles that give you a deeper experience of yourself.

Neale Donald Walsch said it best when I interviewed him for one of my summits. He talked about peace, love and harmony in the world beginning across our dinner table, across the pillow, across the front seats of the car and in the boardrooms and meeting halls of the world. In other words, we demonstrate our Highest Self through our relationships with others.

That being said, I simply invite you to be a source of peace, harmony and love in your relationships. With these as daily, tangible experiences, you'll constantly be calling forth more and more of your Divine expression in the world, and this in turn will bring you closer to an everyday connection with the Highest within you.

As a conscious entrepreneur, a powerful vehicle to "call forth" your Divine gifts is your relationships with your prospects, clients and customers. Sadly, I see many entrepreneurs doing great in regard to their connection to Source, but they completely miss the point when it comes to connecting with their market. Without the connection to your market, you have no business. Which means your gifts are not being shared to the degree they could be, and your business isn't experiencing the success it could be.

I have to admit this is the piece that frustrates me the most because I see it all the time. I meet business owners with incredible gifts and talents, but they're unwilling to get serious about the business of their business (marketing and money) because they say, "The Universe has my back." Yes, that's absolutely true. The Universe does provide. But, money doesn't drop from the heavens; it is given to you through human hands in exchange for the products and services you offer and sell. You've got to pray... and move your feet!

You have a personal responsibility to be a beacon for those you are meant to serve. You must be clear about who your market is and how you can help them. And you need to embrace the monetary value of your product or service and start charging what you're worth.

This, fellow conscious entrepreneurs, is why it's time to take a look at connecting with your market.

What Business Are You In?

Many conscious entrepreneurs fail in business because they're so engrossed in "the work" they neglect doing what it takes to turn "the work" into a successful conscious business. I admit, I made this mistake for many years of my business. Then, one of my mentors made an alarm go off in my head. She said that whatever business I thought I was in, I was wrong. She said no matter what product or service I offered, that wasn't my business. I was in the business of marketing. Why? Because without marketing there is no business. My business changed on that day, because she was right. Marketing (or the lack of it) is what helps your business sink or swim.

Take a deep breath right now. If the thought of marketing makes your stomach turn, then it's time for a wake-up call in this area. No marketing, no business. Know marketing, know business.

I'm going to shed some light on marketing from a conscious perspective and why embracing and even enjoying doing it is so important. First, I want to drive home a point I made earlier about money... because marketing is a tangible tool that will connect you with money.

Money comes to you in exchange for your product or service that solves a problem for your clients and customers. Money does not flow to you just because you meditate for hours, have a vision board on your wall, and have a strong intention to attract clients. Don't get me wrong, all of these intangible/spiritual components are integral to your success. But, you must connect all of your intangible/inner/spiritual work with the physical/tangible/real world through conscious action! It's the integration of spirituality and business in the physical world that leads to more Soul in your business, and more money in your bank! You've got to be blending BOTH worlds to really succeed.

Let's face it, nobody ever had a bag of money drop on their head while they were meditating on the mountain top. But, bags of money have dropped in the hands of entrepreneurs who maintain the vibration of meditating on the mountain top... while working in the physical plane to serve their prospects, customers and clients by helping them solve their problems.

Who Wants Your Product or Service

Unfortunately, many conscious entrepreneurs begin their business with a great idea... a dream. Usually, this idea or dream feels like a spark of inspiration; like they were given the idea to take action and go forth in changing the world. This is good! But, here's the mistake I see happening everywhere. In fact, it's one of the mistakes I've made in the past.

You ignore doing your homework to identify WHO will BUY what you want to sell. And, every single entrepreneur on the planet is in sales. So, it's time to make friends with the reality that you will be selling your product or service. I'm not talking about the "cheesy car salesman" type of selling. I'm talking about offering and selling something you believe in (you) because you know your product or service matches the needs of your prospect or client. It has nothing to do with "closing the deal" but everything to do with "opening a conversation" about the ways in which you can help people.

Many wannabe business owners fall into the trap of not getting clear about who their market is, if there's a demand for their product or service, and the reality that they'll need to market and sell their products or services. They believe the idea they were given was a gift from above and MUST be destined to work in the marketplace, or they wouldn't have been given the idea in the first place.

Here's a glimpse of how this occurs in my own life. I receive a Divine inspiration in the form of a business idea, and immediately I take it to the highest, best possible outcome. In my mind, I easily make money, and have fun fantasizing about income potential. If I help "x" amount of people, sold "x" number of widgets at "x" amount per sale, I'd yield "x" amount of dollars.

However, here's the important part. I enjoy exploring the idea and the fantasy but take action on very few of the ideas. You see, ideas are a dime a dozen for entrepreneurs. We can't help but have new ideas all the time, it's part of how our minds work. But, it's the ideas that are divinely sparked AND match an existing demand in the marketplace where you find the idea that is one in a million.

So, allow the ideas to flow to and through you, and enjoy the fantasy of several successful income streams, but be very careful as to which ideas you pursue. Being strategic in your business is about making these choices. Knowing what your business is will help you say no to what your business is not. You don't want to waste time, money and energy pursuing a great idea that doesn't match a need in the market.

Let me rephrase that. The money, time and energy will not be wasted, because each action you take will teach you valuable lessons, give you new insight, and point you further down your perfect path. So, no matter how challenging an endeavor might be, you will have never wasted time because you and your business will have awakened and evolved from the experience.

Here's something interesting to note about marketing and sales and relating it to your business. The alignment of your product or service and the marketplace may not be apparent at first glimpse. The connection may not be blatantly obvious. This is when you can get creative about how your business evolves and how you position yourself to match a need in the market. Your product or service always remains true to who you are; but how you evolve, promote, position and market yourself—the words you write on your website, the way you package your products and services and communicate your brand position—can be angled to create a match where it wasn't previously obvious.

Let me share an example of this in my own life to illustrate what I'm talking about here. Many years ago, I owned a yoga studio in Los Angeles. This business came forth from my personal passion for yoga as a fitness regimen and as a vehicle to more deeply explore my spirituality. I loved yoga so much, I became a trained and certified teacher and started my yoga business. I knew, first hand, the impact yoga had on people's lives, far beyond the physical realm.

There was something magical about creating a transformational space for others to have an experience of their radiant, divine Self through yoga. This is what kept my business plugging along year after year... creating space for others to experience their own magic. I ended up teaching high-end clients ranging from celebrities like Reba McEntire to 45-year old retired multi-millionaire philanthropists. Even though these clients paid me well and were very rewarding to work with, I didn't have enough of them to support my business.

So, while I enjoyed success in terms of a sense of fulfillment and purpose, financially my yoga business wasn't making it. I was paying a high-end rent in one of the "hottest" neighborhoods in Los Angeles and had a staff of a dozen instructors. There were weeks that I personally taught nearly thirty classes to help make ends meet. But they didn't; my expenses were simply too high for the business to sustain itself and me.

The day I sold the yoga studio I walked out the door for the last time with a huge sense of relief... and a sense of loss. I would miss the magic that had been shared within those studio walls. I would miss the gift of creating the transformational space for my students to experience and know their greatness. Some of my deepest moments of feeling connected to Source were when I sat at the end of a class feeling the profound stillness and Presence in the room after I had guided my students into savasana (final relaxation).

It'll be no surprise to find out that my favorite part of the meetings for my Network for Empowering Women Entrepreneurs was at the end of the meetings when I would lead a powerful guided meditation as all of the women held hands and stood in a large circle around the room.

Again, I was elated by the experience of creating a sacred space for the members to experience their greatness.

By this time in my career, I began to recognize the theme of "creating a transformational space for others to experience their greatness." No matter what I did, this was always at the heart of my passion and had been for years. The problem here was that there wasn't a viable market for a business whose purpose was "to create space." Nobody was looking that up in the yellow pages or running a Google search to pay someone to "hold space."

Thankfully, by now I had learned enough about business and marketing that I started thinking and planning from a strategic perspective. I was smart enough to realize a "holding space" business would never make it. Rather, I began doing my own personal inquiry and a lot of outside research to see how this passion could translate to meeting the needs of a market that already existed and would pay me well.

As a result of this new awareness and my personal and business evolution, I introduced something new and found my "sweet spot." The new business, which I started after filing for bankruptcy, combined my deep passion for facilitating transformational events (which I started in 1997) with my practical and tangible know-how in regard to writing books (which I've done since 2004). This is when I landed on my "holy grail" and pioneered the world of Transformational Authorship.

This work fulfilled my passion for "creating and holding transformational space for others." Yet, it did so for a market segment that I understood; a market that was hungry to learn how to gain clarity, confidence and courage to write an amazing book, while also creating transformation for their business... and in their own life.

With this new business, I feel like I have found my piece of heaven on earth. It meets the four components of a conscious business (make money, make a difference, be who you are, trust in your Divine Plan) and sometimes I feel like I should be paying my clients because I experience such joy in working with them. Everything I've experienced, every new marketing strategy I've learned, every success or challenge I'd had up to this point, makes SENSE now. It all came together because I dared to investigate how my passion could be shared with an already existing market using a business model that worked.

This is what I invite you to look for in your business. Look for the theme of what truly sings to you (for me it was "creating and holding transformational space for others"). Then, be open to seeing how you can do this work for a market that will pay you. For me, the author market was a natural fit. Authors are on a mission to share their message, make a difference, fulfill their calling, and to use their book and book-based-business as a vehicle for their Highest self-expression. They are truly my perfect clients. And, they're a market that, generally speaking, is willing to pay for products and services that bring them closer to their goals and dreams.

It continues to evolve from there. Believe it or not, before this phase of my business growth I had actually shut down my book publishing company due to the tremendous amount of work that went into delivering high-quality, beautifully designed, well written and impeccably edited books.

For several years I had viewed my publishing company as a drain on my energetic and financial resources. Plus, I didn't find it very fulfilling. I had seen it as a commodity-based business focused on delivering a specific good... a book; like most publishers out there. It had been about the book, not necessarily about the author. Then one day when I was hosting a transformational event for 150 authors, they demanded that I open my publishing company again. Their argument was that it was a necessary continuation of the transformation process they had been through to write it. They didn't want to go anywhere else to "birth" their manuscript into a finished, published book.

So, I trusted in the Divine Plan (conscious business component #4) and opened that part of my company again. Having a book is one of the most powerful marketing tools for any business owner. So I realized that offering this service was part of what I needed to do to best serve those transformational authors who understand that a book can be the integration vehicle for the Soul of their business (the message) and the "business" of business (the marketing). Plus, there is a market driven need for ethical, reliable, book publishing service companies that understand the needs of spiritually-minded authors.

Writing a book is like birthing a baby. It is a deeply spiritual experience (even for my clients who don't consider themselves "spiritual"). Authors often feel exposed and vulnerable and have doubts and fears that come up about putting their heart and Soul onto the pages of a book for everyone to see. The most important role I play for aspiring authors is to hold the space of what's possible for them through the process of writing, promoting, and marketing their book. And it's been a miracle to see the shifts that occur as my clients step further into the journey of writing and publishing. Their energy, confidence, clarity and focus dramatically increase and as a result, they experience greater success, often even before the book is done.

My passion for "holding transformational space for others" that began when I hosted my first women's retreat in 1997 carries through everything I do. But now this passion is packaged, promoted and marketed in a way that naturally attracts my ideal clients. So this is what I encourage you to begin to do for your own business. Look for the themes, look for your passions and open yourself up to discovering other ways to creatively package and present your work so it matches the need of a market that will pay you.

My business wouldn't be successful if my headlining benefit was "holding space." Nobody would pay me for that. But, when it's packaged and presented in a way that meets an existing market need, the money easily flows in exchange for the products and services I offer.

After reading my story, I trust you'll now realize how important it is to not just jump at any idea that crosses your mind (like I did with my yoga studio and women's organization). You'll see its worth taking the time to strategize, position and research your business concept before you invest thousands of dollars on hiring a graphic designer, building a website, and developing a new product or service. You're in for a long uphill climb if you don't create a business that fulfills a need in the market.

Now, you may be thinking that you can educate your prospects to realize they do have a need. Then, once you've convinced them of a particular need, pain or want, then you can introduce your product or service as the solution. And yes, you can take this approach. But it takes a lot longer to see results.

I want you to find what many marketers call the low hanging fruit: those prospects who already have a need and are a looking for a solution to their problem or challenge. They are referred to as low hanging fruit because all you need to do is find them and easily pick them from the tree. I know that's not a particularly pleasant analogy, but it illustrates the point.

If you offer a product or service that doesn't have an already existing need, it's like going to the apple orchard and having to find a ladder to climb your way up to the fruit and then balance on your tiptoes, to use a pole to get the fruit down. Now, why would you do that when you can leave the ladder at home, walk up to the tree, and pluck off an apple at shoulder height?

Determine if There's a Market

There are several different ways you can determine if there is a market for your product or service. It can be as simple as a Google search to see if other people have successful business in an area similar to that which you want to pursue. I also recommend you go to the bookstore and look on the shelves to see if there are books on the topic you want to create your business around.

The more similar offerings and businesses you find as you research, the better. Let me say that again. The MORE similar offerings and businesses you find as you research, the better. The reason why it's great to see other businesses succeed in the area you want to pursue or are pursuing is because their success proves to you that there is a market demand for the product or service already in place.

Plus, if you find a company that is already enjoying a certain level of success in the field you are interested in pursuing, you can learn from them and have their company serve as a model. Modeling is done all the time in business. Business owners learn from their peers to see what's working and not working in the marketplace. It's completely ethical to model another business, as long as you don't copy exactly what they're doing. You still need to make it your own. But at least some of the homework and research is already done for you... by them.

I want to offer one warning about modeling, however. And that is to be keenly aware of crossing the line where you lose part of yourself by mistakenly thinking you want to be like "that" person. Whoever you are modeling (including me), please stay away from comparison and getting misaligned in your own identity as your eyes turn toward the person you're modeling.

This can be a very subtle and tricky game to play, telling yourself you're on track when you're really not. I've made this mistake myself in the past, and I know how painful it can be to realize you've been trying to be someone other than yourself. So, yes, go ahead and find people to model, but stay totally aligned and true to who you are.

Narrowing Your Market

Once you've identified there is a viable market for your new idea, or you've evolved your idea to the point where you know there's a market match (like I did) you need to further identify who your target market is. Listen up here. Your target market isn't who you THINK you can get as a client; it's who you WANT to get as a client. You need to become crystal clear on who your target market is, because this knowledge will help you execute a marketing plan that simultaneously attracts those people you feel called to work with and keeps away those people you don't. Your Divine gift is not going to be expressed at its Highest potential when you have clients who drain your energy, don't pay you enough money, make mountains out of molehills and don't respect your time. And, that's exactly what happens when you attract the wrong type of client.

I trust you're beginning to grasp the importance of doing your research first. You may be kicking and screaming that you just want to go for the dream, but take it from one who has done it that way in the past: it's so much better to do the research early on so you can build a business on a solid foundation for long-lasting, joyous success.

ACTION GUIDE EXERCISE #11:

Who is your target market? And, how do you know this market is viable?

Action Guide, page 23
www.thefreedomformula.com/guide

Take Research One Step Further

Once you've identified who your target market is, you can then take your research one step further by surveying those people you've identified as your best potential customers. One method of surveying your target market is simply to create a list of questions and call your prospects (assuming you already have a relationship with them) to request a few minutes of their time. Then, let them know you value their opinion and that you'd like them to help you with your market research by answering a few questions. It helps to give them a small gift in exchange for answering the survey (i.e. a 30-minute consultation, a free-report, downloadable audio, etc.)

The questions you ask should be crafted to provide information about your target market's specific problems and challenges. Having them tell you what challenges they face is invaluable information for you to use in your marketing and promotions. It allows you to learn the language that your target market uses to describe their needs. Remember, the words are how you communicate and connect with your market, so they need to resonate with your market in order to be inspired to act.

Here are a few sample questions to spark ideas. What is the biggest problem or challenge you face in the area of (your expertise)? What have you already done to try to change your situation? What would be possible in your life if you were to overcome this problem or challenge? What do you believe has stopped you in the past from moving past this challenge? What would it mean for you to experience success in this area of your life?

One final thing you'll want to do on this survey call is to introduce your product or service idea and ask for their feedback on what components they'd like to see added or tweaked in order for it to really solve their problem. If you can get your target client to outline what it would take for them to do business with you, you've got some fantastic concepts to implement into your business to make it a "no-brainer" to your market.

Keep in mind this call needs to be pure, meaning that the goal is to gather insight and understanding of your prospective clients' needs. This is not a method to be used to cleverly sell your services. However, it's not unusual for the person to ask for information about your services, because they have felt seen, heard and valued by you. In that case, do share more information with them!

If you have a large group of people you want to survey, the phone call method may not be the most effective. In this case you may prefer to create an online survey to ask your questions. Then, you simply send the link to your target people and ask them to click to your survey and answer the questions. I use www.SurveyMonkey.com or Google Forms for my online surveys.

The incentive for doing this type of research about your idea is that when you've made a "message to market" match—and your ideal client finds you and pays you for services you love to give—it often feels like a joyful, synchronistic Divine appointment. And it can be added to the list of "woo-hoo" moments. You'll feel grateful and blessed to have attracted them and they'll feel grateful and blessed to have found you. There is an energy that occurs between the two of you that flows magnificently when you are doing work you love, with a client you love, and who loves and appreciates you. It's one big love fest, and I can tell you from plenty of experience that it is absolutely worth doing the work to attract your ideal clients.

But along with all of your inner work, it takes some marketing focus and business strategy to pave the way for these Divine connections to occur. Your job is to lay down the path by gaining clarity, matching your passion to a market need, and putting a solid foundation under your business. Once that's done, you can focus more freely on maintaining your light, maintaining your high vibration, and staying connected with your Source. From there, the Universe receives your clear signal that you are truly ready to enjoy a purpose-driven business and a Soul-satisfying life... and it will deliver that for you.

The secret to your success is in your ability to integrate both of these aspects of your business: your spiritual nature (your energy and vibration) and your aligned action in the physical realm. This is where you'll discover the sweet spot in your business.

CHAPTER 3

Design Your Business

(Soul + Connection + Design + I) x E = F

Now that you've discovered the Soul of your business and learned about connecting to Source and to your market, you're ready for the process of designing your business, and your life. I use the word design, rather than plan, because this is the step where you look at the big, broad vision for your business and your life. This is the part where you get to think big, dream your dreams, envision your Highest expression and design the life and the business you want. This step will align you more with the spiritual aspects of your business, whereas implementation (which we'll cover next) pertains more to the specific actions you'll begin taking to have the "rubber hit the road" in the real world.

Before we move forward I want to give you a "heads-up" that with this chapter we are beginning our transition to a more down-to-earth, left-brain energy. Be sure to take all the creative right-brain energy of the previous chapters forward with you as you keep reading.

'How' is None of Your Business

This is one of my favorite statements: "How is none of your business." I first heard it at a workshop in Los Angeles, CA and it's been a mantra of mine ever since. It's a phrase that comes in very handy in this third step. Because when you first begin to design your business, you may be tempted to limit your vision to that which you see as logical and possible from where you stand today. You'll limit yourself to include only those things you know how to do, those things that feel somewhat safe and real.

But for the purpose of this step, I encourage you to ignore "reality" and allow yourself to stretch beyond the limits of your rational, planning, logical mind. Instead, you'll embrace everything you've learned in this book so far about the Soul of your business (you) and your connection to Source and your market, and from there you'll elevate yourself to your God's-eye view, and the infinite abundant supply of the Universe. This is the space in which you'll design your business and your life.

Place Your Order

This concept was made quite popular by the teachings available on the Law of Attraction, which basically means what you think about you bring about. Positive thoughts bring about positive experiences and negative thoughts bring about negative experiences.

That said, imagine you could place an order with the Universe, one that would have the Universe begin to align in such a way that your order would be delivered directly to you. The key to this actually happening is that you are energetically aligned with the order you place.

Let's use a simple example to further explore this. Picture yourself at a restaurant for breakfast. You are excited and happy to have your favorite breakfast— two eggs over easy with toast and a side of fruit. You are 100% energetically aligned with this desire, feeling the excitement and happiness, so you place your order. And fifteen-minutes later your order arrives exactly as you expected.

This is a very basic example, but it's the energy of placing an order with excitement and joy, in alignment with what you desire that allows the order to be delivered. For this delivery is of more important things than breakfast, like what you desire for your business.

If this is a newer concept to you, or you have struggled with this idea, you're not alone. I encourage you to first put your focus on how you want to feel when the order is delivered. Then, as you focus on that feeling, do your best to embrace and embody it. For example, if you want to feel happy and excited then recall a time when you felt happy and excited in the past and let that feeling fill your body, mind and Soul. Stay focused on it until you truly feel that feeling. You may even have a huge smile come across your face!

Then connect with what would deepen the feeling you want to feel... the experience you want to order from the Universe. Once you have this clarity it's time to place your order, which you can do by entering a meditation state, speaking the order out loud, writing it in a letter to the Universe, etc.

Let me add one cautionary note here before proceeding. While it's important to expand your vision, to go beyond that which you know how to do from where you stand today, it's also important that you don't place an order that makes you say to yourself, "You're crazy. That's impossible. Who do you think you are? That'll never happen. You don't deserve that." Because that which you think about, you bring about, and your dream will never be realized. Your order will be deleted by your thoughts.

The vision for your business and your life must feel like a stretch for you, and be out of your current comfort zone, but not so far out that you have a negative association with it. If every time you focus on your vision you instantly connect with feelings of fear, lack or doubt, you're doing yourself a disservice. The life you design for yourself should be one that brings forth feelings of excitement, enthusiasm and ecstatic joy. Not doubt and fear. Remember, you don't have to know how to accomplish the dream. You simply need to be clear about what it is, believe the vision, align your energy with what you desire, keep yourself connected to the Highest within you, and be disciplined to consciously move through the fear, doubt and lack that surface.

Your emotional state is a huge factor in experiencing the business (and life) you desire. So it's important for you to continually seek joy, love, happiness, inner peace, compassion, etc. and stay in the positive feeling emotions.

Use this as a caution to make sure your big vision makes you feel good, rather than "less than."

Speed Matters

You may be asking how to walk this fine line between creating an expansive vision, and not having it bring up doubtful or fearful emotions. I want to share a principle here that will help you walk this line with ease, trust and joy. This is something I learned walking through my own challenges along the entrepreneurial journey. Because, let's face it, it's not easy to create a whole new and exciting vision for your business (and your life) when you don't know where your next month's mortgage (or sometimes your next day's meal) is coming from.

The principle is that of speed. Often, when you think of speed, you likely think of executing an action in the physical world. The speed in which you make a follow-up call, gather information, get a product to market, create an offer, build your website, etc. It's all about the physical, tangible world of "making things happen."

But, the speed I'm talking about here is the speed in which you reconnect to your Source and return to your centered state of being when the feelings of fear, doubt, despair or lack creep in. When you're able to "wake up" and raise your awareness to the Highest within you and in the world, you'll see that whatever is happening in the moment is part of the Divine Plan. You'll be able to manage the lower vibration emotions more easily and get back into alignment with your Higher Self much more quickly.

No matter how difficult a challenge you may be facing, the ability to connect back to your Highest Self quickly is the key to moving through it. I'd like to share a very personal experience that helped me understand this at a deeper level.

Several years ago, I experienced a miscarriage with my second baby when I had wanted nothing more than to bring another child into our family. You can imagine my despair when I miscarried the day after Christmas (after having announced the pregnancy as a gift to our families on Christmas Day). I remember when the loss finally hit me on a deep emotional level four days later; I simply crumbled into a pile of tears on the cold tile floor in my bathroom. I sobbed uncontrollably at the depth of the loss I experienced in miscarrying.

Yet, during my intense and cathartic cry, I somehow found my way to my journal and began to write about what I was experiencing. Through my writing, I was able to reconnect with Source and the feeling that somehow, this too, was happening in alignment with my Divine Plan. I shifted how I related to my loss and despair and gained a new perspective in which to move through this experience… right in the moment I was feeling it the deepest. The speed in which I consciously connected to Source was integral in the rapid and radical transformations I made in my life as a result of this loss in my life.

Another more recent example was when I made the difficult decision to file for bankruptcy. It was one of the lowest times of my life, where at first I couldn't imagine ever getting up and going forth in the pursuit of my dreams again. But through hours of meditation and dedication to wanting to dream, the connection was restored. I found my sense of self, trusted in the unfolding and believed that this too was happening according to Divine Plan and for my Highest good. And things turned around after that connection was made.

I'm sure if you reflect on your own life you can recall those moments where you were slowed down by hitting the bumps in life's road, and more importantly, the moments when you made the choice to not be slowed to a stop but to get back in the game of creating the life you desire. I have a feeling that, like me, when you had those turnaround moments you were able to gain momentum once again in the pursuit of your dreams and the vision you'd always held for yourself and your life.

I trust you're beginning to see how possible it is to create that vision larger than anything you've dreamed of before, while working through and releasing any lower vibration emotions that come along the way.

In the world of high performance sports training they do something called speed drills, where the sole focus of the exercise is to consistently increase speed. Consider this your own personal speed drill. It may take a while to strengthen your speed "muscles" because they may have become atrophied over time. Right now, you get to recondition those "muscles" to respond to heavier and heavier loads. The "load" in this case is the size of your vision, and any lower vibration emotions that may surface if you feel scared or doubtful. The more expansive your vision is, the heavier the load is, which means you have more opportunity to deepen your understanding of yourself, to heal yourself and to do the work to become more energetically aligned with your big vision.

Now that you've prepared your mind and heart for working through the emotions that may come along with your vision, you're ready to begin designing your business, and your life.

How to Identify Your Values

The first step in designing your business (and your life) is to identify your values. This is the foundation on which everything will grow. The reason your values are so important is because your values support you in experiencing long-term sustainable success, as well as keep you from compromising yourself for the sake of your dreams. If you design your business with disregard for your values, you're setting yourself up for a long, challenging road that won't be any fun. There is no dream unless it allows you to experience your values each and every day.

BusinessDictionary.com shares this definition of values: Values: In general: Important and enduring beliefs or ideals shared by the members of a culture about what is good or desirable and what is not. Values exert major influence on the behavior of an individual and serve as broad guidelines in all situations.

For example, one of my values is family which, for me, includes being a present mom and a loving and supportive wife. Considering that I work at home, it would be easy for me to be in the office from 8 AM to 10PM. But that wouldn't honor my value of family. So, I make it a point to drive my daughter to the bus stop, cook family dinners and eat together at our kitchen table, have "no phone time" that's filled with connection and conversation, enjoy a few vacations a year, rarely work on weekends, etc.

Another fun thing I do to connect with my value of family is to bake pies. I never made a pie in my life until I met my husband; he's got a real hankering for pie, so I made it a hobby to learn how to make them. Lucky for me, I discovered that it really is 'easy as pie.' There's something about baking a pie that nurtures my husband, our family and myself. Baking a pie instantly connects me with the joy of being a wife and mother.

Anyway, the thing to remember about designing a business (and a life) that supports your values is that you may work at a different pace than other entrepreneurs who sacrifice their values for the sake of their business. This is not what conscious business is about. So, be prepared to possibly move a bit slower than your colleagues who work 60-80 hours a week. And know that you are on a journey and all is happening in Divine right time. You don't need to keep up with anyone. This is all about what works for YOU!

So, now I invite you to reflect on your own values. Notice (without judging yourself) if there is disparity between your values and your current life, and become aware of those things you'd like to experience differently than you are now. Your values are there as guideposts to anchor you in your belief of what's important… while you work toward realizing your dreams for your business and your life.

ACTION GUIDE EXERCISE #12:

This exercise invites you to identify your core values.

Action Guide, page 24
www.thefreedomformula.com/guide

To help you get started, here's a list of some common life values I see in my clients. Which of these resonate with you?

Accomplishment	Family	Leadership
Adventure	Freedom	Learning
Beauty	Friendship	Love
Business	Fun	Meaning
Community	Gratitude	Money
Creativity	Health	Peace
Expression	Honesty	Personal Growth
Faith	Integrity	Prosperity

Respect
Self-Care
Solitude
Spirituality
Success
Trust
Wisdom

When you live your life as a reflection of your values, and take actions to LIVE your values, your ability to manifest increases greatly. Because when your values are reflected throughout your life, you have more energy and enthusiasm for all that you do, and this increased energy and enthusiasm become a magnet for you to attract more of what you desire, which leads to more energy and more enthusiasm. Living your life as a demonstration of your values becomes the base of a continual upward spiral toward your Highest and best good.

How to Focus on Your Priorities

Now that you've identified your values, the next step in designing your business is to identify your priorities. Your priorities will help you make decisions about your business and your life to determine what takes precedence. Entrepreneurs tend to think that everything is equally important and/or urgent and take on more than they can handle. This is the very thinking that keeps entrepreneurs stagnant, not making measurable progress in any area.

Being spread too thin because everything is "important" is a sure-fire road to burnout, frustration and financial strain. To succeed as a conscious entrepreneur, you need to identify your highest priorities and let them guide you when you feel yourself being pulled off track.

For the sake of this exercise, I'd like you to identify your top five priorities only. If your list gets longer than that, it can become overwhelming. Narrowing down to your top five makes it short, simple and powerful.

Your priorities are based on your values, but taken one step further. You create your priorities in a hierarchical order with those higher up on the list being the most important. The reason you rank them in order is so you can use them to help you make important decisions in your business and your life. For example, let's say your highest priority is your health; you can use this as a motivator to wake up just a little bit earlier to get your workout in before the day starts. The interesting thing about this is if you consistently say you're going to get up early to exercise and don't, then health may not be your top priority, even though you say you want it to be. If the five priorities you identified are truly your top priorities, they'll cause you to make a change in your life.

When you are fully committed to living by your priorities, (and not only wishful thinking), you're telling the Universe you're serious about living the life you say you want. Your priority-based actions in the physical world act like rocket-fuel for your dreams to be realized.

Use your priorities as a way to show the Universe you are committed to living your best life, so you can be the Highest and fullest expression of yourself. It's when you live in this place of full self-expression that your Divine gifts shine and your contribution to the world is magnified exponentially. So, if you've ever thought of priorities as something that "aren't for you," it's time to rethink your relationship to them. Because when all is said and done, living by your priorities is a way to experience more of your Divine Self!

Now, I don't know about you, but when I learned about priorities in terms of my business, nobody ever told me they were a way for me to connect with my Divine Self. But that's what they are. Just like your values, they serve as your guideposts to help you be fully who you are and attract that which you desire.

Now that you understand the importance of your priorities, it's time for you to identify yours.

ACTION GUIDE EXERCISE #13:

This exercise invites you to identify your top five priorities, based on your values.

Action Guide, page 24
www.thefreedomformula.com/guide

Go ahead and review your values list and from that, write down your top five priorities. Once you've written your five priorities, take some time to review them and see if they are in the right order for you. If the order of priorities shifts after some reflection, shift the order on your list to reflect what is true for you.

This list of priorities, in order of importance, is an important tool in keeping you focused and on track. If one day you're bombarded with distractions and are pulled off track, you can refer back to this list to regain your focus and to bring peace to your decision-making process. During a hectic day I've said to myself, "There are so many things to do, I don't know where to start." No more! I just refer to this list and the answer is simple: start with the priorities. And, now you can, too.

Creating Your Lifestyle Vision

Your lifestyle vision is one that includes everything about your life. Too often, when you get into traditional business visioning, this element is completely left out of the equation. For the conscious entrepreneur this is actually where it has to begin. Your business is integral in your life; it is an expression of who you are in the world. You can't separate your business from your life... which is why your lifestyle vision is so important.

It's the integration of the whole that you're creating in this step. I think this is why so many corporate employees decide to start their own business; they became tired of having to compartmentalize the whole of their life for the sake of the part that was about climbing higher up the corporate ladder. The view from the top of the ladder is bleak, when you don't see your family or friends and you have no connection to your authentic self.

The concept of integration isn't new. It has been around for ages, but it's finally coming to the forefront as our culture realizes that there is so much more to success than the acquisition of money. Money, in and of itself, is ungratifying. It's a piece of paper with numbers on it. But, when money is used to help you express more of who you are in the world, then money is serving its purpose: for you to be more of who you are, for your gifts to shine more brightly in the world and for you to make a larger positive impact on the people whose lives you touch. That is what money is for. I wrote this book specifically for the ever-growing population of entrepreneurs who want to create a successful business and live their life according to their Highest aspirations for a fully integrated, fully expressed, and financially abundant life.

Your lifestyle vision can include the generalities of your business (because that is an integral part of your life), but leave the detailed vision for your business to the next step. For now, simply focus on your vision for your whole life.

This vision, when complete, should evoke positive emotions and increase your energy and enthusiasm for your life!

Below I've listed several areas that you may want to consider when creating your big vision. As you write about these areas, include the details of them, especially how you want to experience yourself FEELING.

Here are some areas to consider when writing your

lifestyle vision:	Daily ritual
Home	Environment
Family	Recreation
Community	Fitness
Friends	Social Involvement
Geographic location	Giving Back/Philanthropy
Emotional state of being	Personal development
Expressions of love	Business growth
Travel	Financial goals
Spirituality	Emotional well-being

ACTION GUIDE EXERCISE #14:

Write the vision for your life/lifestyle.

Action Guide, page 25
www.thefreedomformula.com/guide

If you'd like to take this exercise one step further, create a vision board to be a physical representation of your written lifestyle vision. Then hang your vision board on a wall in your home or office and reflect on it regularly. While you take time to reflect, do so with a feeling of positive energy coursing through your being as if everything on your vision board were real in your life today.

This or Something Better

As you create your vision, keep in mind the element of the unknown and allow room for miracles and unexpected blessings to come into your vision. What I mean by this is even though your vision may feel big, huge, exciting and awesome to you, still, God sees so much more. It's impossible to know just what miracles and gifts are in store for you. So, to make room for (and invite) the unknown, write this statement at the end of your vision: This or Something Better! This statement is like hanging a sign that says, "I'm open to receive that which You see for me, even bigger and better than I can see for myself. Thank You in advance for the gifts You'll bestow on me."

Creating Your Business Vision

Your business vision is created within the context of your lifestyle vision. Your lifestyle vision is about the whole of your life, and your business vision is specific to your business.

The more clarity you have about your business vision, the more energy you'll have to consciously create and attract everything you desire for this vision to be realized. Until you experience the power of clarity, it's like a ship sailing through the night with a captain without a navigation system, who has no idea where the ship is, or where it's going. As soon as the captain knows the ship's latitude and longitude, and where it's going, the navigation provides directions right to port. The same goes for your business. Clarity is power!

I know from personal experience the cost of not being clear about my business. In fact, I struggled for years when I went to networking meetings (or anywhere) and people asked me what I did. I'd often stumble on my words, saying something different every time I answered the question, and whatever I said landed like a "flat-line" on the other person's ears. It's a horrible feeling. I believe part of this struggle came from trying to fit in with everyone else and model that which I'd seen as successful, but not quite right for me. The first step of *The Freedom Formula* is about discovering the Soul of YOUR business because clarity on this helps you gain clarity on everything else.

As you develop your business vision, do your best to describe in detail what you do, how you do it, how you feel when doing it, how others help you, how your clients' lives change, how you impact those around you, how it feels to serve, etc. Just like in your lifestyle vision, write all of this down with the belief the Universe may have something bigger and better in store for you. So don't hesitate to be specific, to include numbers, to anticipate gross revenues, bottom-line profit, expansion plans or anything else that feels concrete. Just know that you're not limited to the scope of your own imagination. There is a greater force in partnership with you for your Highest good. Thus, it's important to include at the end of your business vision the words: This or Something Better.

Take as much time and write as many words as necessary to paint a clear picture of the business you are creating, ensuring that this vision evokes a feeling of enthusiasm and excitement within you. These positive emotions need to be associated with the vision for it to have power. As with your lifestyle vision, if you experience fear, lack or doubt as you create your dream business, take a break to reconnect with Source energy and your peaceful, powerful Self. Once you realize you're not creating your vision alone, it gets easier to resonate with it. If it still feels scary, then shift the vision a bit so you experience positive emotions when you reflect upon it.

There's space in your action guide to write the broad, expansive and exciting vision for your business.

Once you've completed that, consider how each of the business aspects listed next fit with that grand vision.

Products and Services Offerings

Target Audience

Scalability

Product Funnels

Your Network

Support Team

Home-based or Bricks and Mortar

What You Do vs. What Your Team Does

Number of Hours you work

Number of clients .

Sales process

Customer Service

Branding

Speaking

Publicity

Visibility

Marketing

Web Presence

Business Development

Your business vision is a way of seeing your true Self through your business. When you are clear about what it is you want for your business, and what you provide for your clients and customers, success comes much more easily. Because clarity is power. The more crystal clear you are about your vision, the more you can focus your energy on experiencing your vision, the more you'll connect with the clients and customers you're meant to serve and the more energy you'll have in pursuing your vision. Your vision begins a positive upwards spiral that continually draws you forward on your entrepreneurial journey. Plus it makes it easier to say no to the things that may distract from the vision.

So, take some time right now to write your vision for your business. Additionally, if you would like to create a vision board to reflect on regularly, take some time to do that.

ACTION GUIDE EXERCISE #15:

Write your vision for your business.

Action Guide, page 26
www.thefreedomformula.com/guide

CHAPTER 4

Implement Your New Business Vision

〜〜〜

(Soul + Connection + Design + Implementation) x E = F

Ahhh, so now it's time to bring the first three steps of *The Freedom Formula* into the physical realm with a concrete written plan you'll implement. This step is where you bring the intangible/invisible/universal principles into reality through your action. For some conscious entrepreneurs, this is a difficult step because you'd rather create, meditate, dream or read an inspiring book than plan for business success. For others, this is your favorite part. Whatever previous notion you've had about business planning, set it aside for now and allow this process to help you bring shape and tangible form to your visions. This process is what makes implementation easy.

Earlier in my entrepreneur career, I found planning to be a challenge. I operated my business for years without a written plan. I kept working on project after project, and spent time working "in" my business, instead of "on" my business. Perhaps like you, I wasn't going to a bank for financing, wasn't seeking venture capital and just didn't see the point in writing one of those formal business plans that bankers and venture capitalists wanted. Those types of plans didn't feel right to me. I wanted a plan that wasn't just words on paper someone else needed to see, but rather a guide to point me in the right direction in case I got off course…. and ensure I took aligned action to realize my vision.

I used to be a proponent of "winging it," but I'm not so much anymore. Though winging it comes in handy if you tend to procrastinate or feel stopped by fear that you're not prepared enough, winging it can cause you to take actions toward your goals even before you feel fully ready. There are two sides of the coin to balance here. In winging it you don't want to naively go forward with a plan that has no viable market (see Chapter 2), nor do you want to get so wrapped up in the short-term project in front of you that you forget how it fits into the whole of your business. That's what happened to me; I would experience success with one project or another, but I didn't have a larger view of how each project worked in relation to the overall business. I was continually starting from scratch on every project because I didn't know where I was going. And, let me tell you, that type of unplanned work takes a ton of energy. It's like having to "lift off" over and over again. Which is why I now love having a plan: each piece of my business makes sense now and my projects, products and services are all related to and supportive of the others.

Research shows that writing something down increases the likelihood of it being realized. Most of the motivational speakers out there talk about this specifically in relation to goals. They tell you to write down your goals in order to make them happen. And, I agree, but take it one step further. And that is to write down your plan so all of it can happen. This or something better.

What I discovered when I began talking with many of my colleagues is they didn't have a plan either. So, we decided to buddy up and work on a plan while holding each other accountable for implementing it. I'll share with you the resource we used to guide us through the process. We used the book, *One Page Business Plan* written by Jim Horan. The planning process was surprisingly easy when we followed his guidelines step by step. If you don't have the book yet, I encourage you to pick it up.

Another type of planning tool I use is my very own "Sticky Note Business Plan." I knew I struck a chord with this planning method by the response I got to an article I wrote about it. My Sticky Note Business Plan is a simple and fun tool you can use anytime, anywhere, to keep your business pointing in the right direction.

Birthing Your Plan

1) Gather Your Planning Supplies

Thankfully, you won't need fancy computer software or heavy reference books to write your plan. All you'll need is a wall (or floor), six large pieces of paper or poster board, three pads of small sticky notes, scotch tape, a note pad, a Sharpie marker and a pen. It'll also help to have a quiet place and a few hours of time to enjoy this process. You may even want to light your favorite candle and play some relaxing music or invite a friend or colleague to join you for a planning day.

2) Lay out Your Plan

Tape the six pieces of paper or poster board up on the wall. Once they are up on the wall, grab your notepad. Sit down for a few minutes and quietly think about the aspects of your business you want to plan. For example: do you need to design a new product, produce an event, create a marketing plan or launch a new website? Do you need a timeline for the next three years of your business or only the next year? Is it time to introduce a new service?

Use your notepad to collect all of your ideas and decide which of the main ideas you want to use as the six categories in your plan. Next, transfer the six categories, one each, to six separate sticky notes, using your Sharpie marker. Then, stick one note on the top center of each piece of paper/poster board... so each is labeled for one of your six topics.

3) Download Your Ideas

Here comes the fun part. Get your pen and sticky notes and begin to write down every single idea or task that comes to mind for each category. Don't edit or censor any ideas. Simply write them down and stick them on the paper for that category. Try to stay with one category at a time as best you can. But if other ideas do keep coming to mind, write them down and pop that sticky note on the appropriate paper/board. Let the ideas flow and enjoy the process of getting everything on paper.

4) Organize Your Ideas

So, now that your ideas are on the papers, begin to organize them. Look for themes, sequences, and categories of items. Physically move the sticky notes on the paper to group ideas together. (It's totally okay if you need a few pieces of paper for one category.) Sometimes I'll organize ideas by timeline, sometimes I'll organize by concept... you can organize them in the way that makes sense to you.

5) *Put It All Together*

Now, step back and take a look at your whole plan. After going through this process, you may discover that some items need to move higher on your priority list; while other ideas may need to be dropped from your plan completely. The right things to do (and the order in which to do them) will surface now that you have the whole plan in front of you. Next, rearrange the papers so the highest priority category is at the left side of the wall and the lower priority one is to the right side of the wall. Finally, transfer your highest priority tasks to your calendar to make sure you begin executing your plan.

6) *Keep Going*

As you make progress with your plan, continually re-evaluate where you are and keep moving forward with your projects. And, if you feel called to do so, once you've completed a project and removed the sticky note, you can add a new project to "the wall."

Personally, once I complete a task from one of my categories, I remove the sticky notes related to that task, so I can visually see the space open up as I make progress with my plan. You may enjoy doing the same thing.

Now that you know how to write your Sticky Note Business Plan, you'll discover it's actually FUN to work on your plan. And, it's a huge asset to your business, because it's easy to implement.

Time Frame

I encourage you to keep the timeline for your Sticky Note Business Plan to one year. Your business will evolve a lot over the course of a year, as will you. Trying to write a detailed plan for more than a year can be quite an undertaking, especially when you consider how accelerated the rate of growth is in today's world. Your overall lifestyle and business vision adequately communicate the long-term vision for your business and your life, so it's really not necessary here.

Guess what I'm going to tell you to write at the bottom of each poster board sticky note plan? Correct: This or Something Better. As with everything in conscious business, the Divine element needs to be included, or you've missed the point. This is about planning for what you can see for yourself and your business, while remaining completely open to receiving something bigger and better from the Universe.

The plan moves you forward exponentially because with each step you implement the more you are telling the Universe you're serious about this, and you're willing to do what it takes in the physical realm to achieve your goals.

Your plan is like a fluid, ever-evolving dance between the spiritual and the practical that unfolds more beautifully with each and every step.

A Heads-up

Let me give you a "heads-up" here for a moment. As you implement more in the physical realm, you may encounter more blocks and barriers in the form of fear and doubt. The closer you come to achieving a goal, you may experience something Maria Nemeth calls "trouble at the border" in her book *The Energy of Money*. "Trouble at the border" occurs when you get closer to moving something from the invisible realm of possible into the physical realm of reality. This is a natural part of your conscious business evolution and something to welcome with open arms when it happens. Because it means you are approaching the border, and therefore very close to seeing your dream become real.

If you find yourself struggling with fear or doubt as you approach the reality of your dream, I invite you to consider this: there are no mistakes and you cannot fail. You read that right. There are no mistakes and you cannot fail. Each step you take in the fulfillment of your dreams either leads you towards your goal or teaches you valuable information to know if or when to redirect your plan.

This is called learning in action. It is, by far, the fastest way to learn anything in business or in life. One of my favorite sayings is "you can't steer a parked car." The sooner you get into action, the sooner you will realize if you are on track or not, and if you need to course correct. You will save more time, money and energy by getting the ball rolling to see what happens rather than engaging in procrastination, planning and perfecting, but never actually taking action. This is why I recommend my Sticky Note Business Plan. It's not about perfect planning, it's about making planning fun and something you can easily take strides in implementing.

Your actions are the way in which you show the Universe you are ready for what's next. Approach each action with the openness to receive whatever gifts you are given. I trust many times you'll receive the gift of reassurance by having the Universe fully support your action. Other times you'll receive the gift or wisdom and redirection as you are pointed down a different direction with deeper understanding and clarity.

Throw Your Book Bag 'Over the Fence'

I often tell my clients to throw their book bag over the fence. By this I mean take action, do something. Make a commitment to implement! Once your proverbial book bag is tossed over the fence (you commit to action) you've got to go get your book bag (do what you said you'd do).

An example in my own life was when I made a huge financial commitment to host a transformational writing retreat in Costa Rica. I had never done an international retreat before, had never been to the resort location, nor did I have anyone signed up to go to this event at the time I signed the contract and put down a large deposit. It felt risky and scary but I knew that if I made this commitment (threw my book back over the fence) that I'd take action to have a successful event (go get my book bag). And that's exactly what happened. By the time I made my final payment to the resort, there were 22 amazing people joining me to write their transformational books on the beach in Costa Rica. It was amazing for us all!

For those of you who truly find yourself gripped by procrastination, here are a couple of ways to get your book bag over the fence and implement! Whenever I find myself in this situation, I follow one of these two ways to stop procrastinating and get going. Before you read further, think about one project that's been on your "To Do" list for quite a while. Then, after you discover the following tools, choose one of the tools to move your project from procrastination to realization.

Make a Financial Commitment

You've probably heard the expression, "Put some skin in the game." The "skin" this phrase refers to is money. So, if you're on the fence about taking action on something, one of the best ways to break your inertia and start moving is to make a financial commitment to your goal. When you've got "skin" in the game, you have a good reason to get going... every DOLLAR is a reason!

Many entrepreneurs, myself included, invest in coaches, mentors and experts to help us achieve our goals. Something happens when you make a financial commitment by paying for guidance along the way... you want to get your money's worth! So if you're the type of person who wants to get YOUR money's worth, invest in a coach/teacher/mentor whose fee is a little outside of your comfort zone. Stretching beyond your comfort zone can be a significant step to catapult you into your next transformation personally and professionally.

For some people $50 is a stretch, for others $50,000 is a stretch. Whatever feels like a stretch to you, make that investment in yourself... as well as a commitment to get your money's worth.

Make a Public Commitment

Another way to end procrastination is to make a public commitment. A public commitment is one where you tell other people what you're going to do, and when you're going to do it. When you have a commitment to other people, the responsibility to honor your word will get you in gear to finally accomplish the project you've been putting off. As a conscious entrepreneur, your integrity is one of your most valuable assets, so this tool can be a good one to get you in action. Do what you say you're going to do!

Here are a few examples of how you can make a public commitment:

- Schedule a seminar you want to teach, schedule the date and announce it
- Announce to your community something you're GOING to offer.
- Say "yes" to a speaking engagement before you have the speech written.
- Say "yes" to anything that fits in your business plan... BEFORE you're "ready."
- Pre-sell a product prior to its completion.
- Tell people you're going to do something, and THEN figure out how to do it.

Warning: Public commitments are not for the faint of heart. These types of commitments can be scarier than putting skin in the game. If you make a public commitment to stop your procrastination, be prepared to possibly "sweat it out" a few times before it all comes together. On the other hand, this is a GREAT way to get yourself in gear.

Now that you know some ways to end procrastination, go back to the task that came to mind at the beginning of this section. Decide which of the above tools you'll use to end your procrastination and implement once and for all.

Remember, your intentions in the invisible world need to be matched with actions in the visible world, in order to see results. Be a decisive, action-oriented person who implements… knowing that your action is part of the unfolding of your Divine Plan.

Take Action by Saying "No"

Remember the T-shirt saying, "What part of NO don't you understand?" I used to get a kick every time I saw that T-shirt because I was the type of person who found the word "no" very difficult to say. And there were people who wore it proudly who took pride in saying "no." Thankfully, I've come a long way with regards to the word "no" and while you'll never see me wearing a "no" T-shirt, you will hear me say "no" more often than I could before. I bring this up to you now, because "no" is considered an action word. In fact, some of the most challenging actions you'll take in your business (and life) will be to say "no" to something or someone.

But for many conscious business owners, your sensitivity and awareness of others significantly increases the ease in which you say "yes"... and sometimes you don't even entertain the thought of saying "no, thank you." It's understandable you want to help others, and be of service to them, but saying "yes" when you really feel like saying "no" sends conflicting, confusing and unclear messages to the Universe.

So, why does it serve your Highest good to say "no?" Because every time you say "no" to what you don't want, you're saying "yes" to what you do want. Saying "no" to one thing adds energy to another thing you desire more. "No" is a great way to send a clear message. It shows you're 100% willing to "put your money where your mouth is" and make decisions that support your Highest good.

When you take into consideration the plan you've developed for your business, you'll discover that having a plan makes it much easier to know what to say "yes" to and what opportunities to turn down. And, just like any other muscle, the more you exercise your "no" muscle, the easier it is to use.

The biggest barrier you'll face in saying "no" is the fear of letting others down. When that fear leads you, you let yourself down. You're not supposed to do things that don't feel right to you. Remember, your job as a conscious entrepreneur is to keep your emotions and energies up into the higher vibrational realms, and it's impossible to do that if you're always doing things you wish you didn't have to do. So, start saying "no." If it doesn't feel right to say "yes," it's not in alignment with you. You'll know when it's the right time to say "yes" because it'll increase your energy, fill your heart with joy and bring a sense of satisfaction to your Soul.

As you take action and make more commitments, you just may discover that you need to commit to saying "no", too. You get the idea? "No" is a strategy that can help you fulfill your business vision because of everything that "no" actually says "yes" to.

ACTION GUIDE EXERCISE #16:

Write a list of things you need to say "no" to.

Action Guide, page 27
www.thefreedomformula.com/guide

Make Every Day Count

Now that you know the importance of having a plan, making commitments, ending procrastination, and implementing (even if that means saying "no"), it's time to take a look at how you can boil this down to the everyday events of your life. After all, those things you choose to do each day are the things that will make up the fabric of your existence.

If you've ever taken a goal setting or time management seminar, you know the importance of writing things down and planning the activity of your days to help you achieve your end goal. I needed my daily planner almost more than I needed food, water, and sleep to survive. If I left home without it, I'd go back home to get it because "my life" was in that planner. It was somewhat of a dysfunction and a joking point among my friends because if they saw me, they saw my maroon leather encased daily planner in hand. In hindsight, I think my hefty daily planner filled with tons of things to do every day was a way for me to boost the low self-esteem I had at that point in my life.

Anyway, I was so addicted to daily planning and writing down a gazillion things on my daily "To Do" list that I was a very late adapter when it came to going digital with my daily planner. Finally, when I did go digital with a Palm Pilot (remember those?), it was awesome! It was easier to organize my overflowing "To Do" list and feel even more significant because I could easily manage multiple "To Do" lists at the touch of a button. Heaven, right?

Not exactly. It wasn't until my Palm Pilot broke that I realized how much my "To Do" list obsession was stopping me from achieving anything. At the end of the day, yes, I could check off a bunch of things on my list, but they didn't mean anything. Nor did those items on my list propel me forward toward my goals. They just kept me busy and feeling very important because I had so much to do. So, when my planner went kaput, I decided not to replace it, and I started managing a much smaller "To Do" list with much more important tasks. The results? I achieved my goals faster and easier than before. I didn't waste time on unimportant tasks, I got focused on what really mattered, and what would have the most impact on my business and my life.

Today, my average daily task list has only three items on it. Coming from someone who used to consider anything less than ten items an unsuccessful day, I've made some real progress.

You see, the fewer things you do, the more your energy is focused on a particular result. Whereas, the more you do, the more scattered your energy. And, scattered energy doesn't send a clear signal to the Universe to support your endeavors. Instead, scattered energy puts the Universe on hold because it doesn't know how to respond to you.

That being said, I encourage you to break your big plan down into daily actions. Each day include only two to three action items you consider high priority tasks, the ones that, at the end of the day, give you a sense of accomplishment from making progress toward your goals. This strategy alone will drastically shift your focus and energy, and as a result, the Universe's ability to favorably respond to you by sending you an abundance of opportunities, and as a result, more money in your bank.

Plan to Take Care of Yourself

As a seasoned veteran of the fitness industry, I'd be remiss to not take this opportunity to talk with you about planning to take care of yourself. The plans you have for your business and your life don't mean anything if you don't have your health.

Your physical well-being contributes to your emotional well-being, which contributes to your spiritual well-being, which contributes to your physical well-being. It's all interconnected. That's one of the great things about being a conscious entrepreneur: you get to awaken to every aspect of your life and fully integrate it into one unified, integrated life that is lived to its fullest potential.

This is not a fitness book, so I'm not going to be long-winded about taking care of yourself. Here are a few general guidelines wise to follow in maintaining the health needed to pursue (and enjoy) your dreams.

- Exercise at least three times per week.
- Eat sensible, well-balanced meals.
- Get enough sleep (average person needs seven to eight hours).
- Drink 64 ounces of water per day.
- Enjoy personal downtime.
- Reduce intake of soda, caffeine, sugar, processed foods and alcohol.
- Take time to relax and rest (other than sleeping).
- Be proactive about taking charge of your health.

Here are a few of my personal favorites when it comes to maintaining my health:

- Eat an apple a day.
- Cook nearly all of my meals at home.
- Hula hoop to my favorite tunes.
- Walk around the park near my house.
- Go dancing.
- Practice yoga.
- Drink organic herbal tea and alkaline water.
- Sleep seven to eight hours per night.
- Relax in an Epsom salt and lavender oil bath.
- Escape to the spa once monthly for a day of relaxation.
- Get outside as much as possible to enjoy nature.

That's all I'm going to say about planning for your health. I trust these few ideas either helped confirm that you're already taking good care of your health or renewed your commitment to take action toward improving the way in which you love and care for your physical self. Simply keep in mind that you are a spiritual being expressed in the form of a physical body. As a conscious entrepreneur you have an obligation to keep your Soul's home in good health, so you can more fully (and more easily) express the ever glowing, ever expanding Divine light within.

Implement, Implement, Implement

The most important concept you need to draw from this chapter is to get into action in the physical, tangible world. Creating and executing your plan, on every level, is your roadmap to being everything you are meant to be, doing those things you are destined to do and having those things (and experiences) that are divinely meant for you.

Remember, the person who meditates on the mountain trying to manifest a million dollars never had a bag of money drop on her head. It's imperative you take all of your spiritual understandings and Divine aspirations and show the Universe you are serious about seeing them realized. This happens through the actions you take (action is a powerful form of prayer) and the consciousness/intention you have when taking those actions.

Please do not take this chapter lightly. This is where the rubber hits the road. It's as if you were pregnant with your Highest and best potential, but until you go through "labor" (implementing your plan), your Divine gifts within will not get birthed into the real world. And, as I mentioned earlier, one of the biggest benefits to executing your plan and taking action is the gift of learning in action. So, before you begin the next chapter on realizing your dreams, take a moment to schedule time to focus on your plan and take steps to birth your new business vision.

It doesn't matter if the things you'll implement are large or small. They could be as simple as going to a networking event, or as complex as developing a new program or service. Only you know what is most critical for you to implement.

ACTION GUIDE EXERCISE #17:

Write down the five most important things for you to implement—to help make your life and business vision reality. Include the date that action will be complete.

Action Guide, page 28
www.thefreedomformula.com/guide

CHAPTER 5

Maintain Your Energy and Realize Your Dreams

(Soul + Connection + Design + Implementation)
x Energy = F

The final step to *The Freedom Formula* is the glorious experience of maintaining your energy and realizing your dreams. This step of the formula is the opposite of the previous chapters on implementing your new business vision. This chapter is about opening yourself up to receive the fruits of your emotional, spiritual and physical "labor." We'll cover two primary concepts in this chapter. The first is how to energetically open yourself up to receive your portion of the infinite abundant supply of the Universe. The second is how to help you maintain the highest energy possible to continue your journey of personal transformation, spiritual connection and business success.

Be Open to Receive

For many conscious entrepreneurs, we're used to giving, serving and being there for others. Receiving, on the other hand, doesn't come as naturally. To give you an example, recall a moment when you received a genuine compliment from a friend. What did you do? Chances are you downplayed whatever they acknowledged in you. Compliments are rarely received with a simple "thank you." There's usually something attached to it to diminish the significance of that which you're being complimented on.

Perhaps it comes from a society that told you "don't be too full of yourself," "it's not nice to brag," and the list could go on and on. Culturally we are not raised to hold our heads high and say, "thank you, I appreciate your acknowledgment and I agree with you." Whatever the reason is for this dismissal of receiving compliments doesn't matter. What matters is that you become aware of how you personally stand in this regard and begin accepting compliments in a completely new way.

So, why are we talking about compliments, and how to accept them? Because it's a lesson in Receiving 101. How you receive a compliment is indicative of your overall ability to receive. The next time someone gives you a compliment, whether it's for your fantastic shoes, a stellar speech, or your ability to listen and support, practice simply saying "thank you." And stop there! Do not justify, do not explain how you got the shoes on sale, or didn't really think your speech was very good, or that it was "nothing" to be there for a friend. These are all ways to show the Universe that you are not ready to receive... anything. How can you receive money, love, or fame, whatever you desire, if you can't receive a compliment on your new shoes?!

Another fantastic way to exercise your receiving muscle is around the good green stuff. No, not wheat grass... we're talking about money here! Have you ever done this? You receive a payment for one of your products or services, and rather than expressing your deepest gratitude for receiving the money (even if it's $20), you dismiss the money with an instant thought of how it's not enough. Well, what kind of message are you sending to the Universe when you do this? How can you expect to attract thousands of dollars, perhaps millions of dollars, if you have no appreciation for 20 dollars?

I can only share this with you because I've been guilty of this myself. There have been times when I would attract thousands of dollars, and the first thought in my mind was, "it's not enough, I need more." Rather than, "thank you!" It was like a magnet with a negative force that repelled money away from me. And it will be for you, too. I've even learned to stop and pick up pennies I see lying on the ground with the awareness that those pennies remind me to be grateful for receiving even a one cent. It's a sign of the abundance in the Universe. There's a reason why "in God we trust" is printed on our money!

So, now I ask you to take an honest assessment of how you receive money. Do you receive $1,000 differently than $10? What do you need to do to have the same feeling of gratitude no matter what the amount is? This is your exercise. Begin looking for pennies on the ground, and picking them up with a feeling of gratitude, as if it's a "God wink" especially for you. If you receive checks, when you endorse them write the words "thank you" on the check.

If you have an Internet based business and you never physically hold the money, but simply see a receipt that a deposit has been made to your bank account, take a moment, when you get the receipt, to acknowledge receiving that money as if it were handed to you. You can simply say the words "thank you" out loud. If you prefer, you can add a statement like this, "I gratefully receive the money. I acknowledge this money as a Divine gift and accept it with joy and gratitude." Notice the difference between this statement and the words, "It's not enough, I need more."

Now, make a conscious choice to appreciate every dollar (and every penny) that you receive. And, trust that the Universe hears you loud and clear.

Once you embrace receiving compliments and money, you will find it easier to identify so many other things you can express gratitude for receiving. To help, here are a few of my favorite gifts to exercise my receiving muscle:

- A long hug from my husband
- A gentle breeze caressing my face
- Morning cuddles with my two cats
- A "just called to say hi" conversation with a friend
- A thank you note from a client
- No line at the grocery store
- Reading just the right article at just the right time
- Someone letting me into a lane of traffic
- Hearing the word "yes" when I ask for help

Begin looking at your life through the eyes of receiving. The more you authentically express gratitude for receiving, the more you will be given. Receiving is like a receptacle that gets bigger and bigger the more you consciously receive.

ACTION GUIDE EXERCISE #18:

Write a list of at least 25 'gifts'
you are grateful for receiving.

Action Guide, page 28-29
www.thefreedomformula.com/guide

Eventually, you'll experience the feeling of your "cup runneth over" because you'll begin receiving so much, your Self and your business will need to catch up with all that you are receiving. Which brings me to the next point.

How to Manage Growth

As a conscious entrepreneur, one of the goals for your business is growth. The more your business grows, the more people you serve, the more lives you impact, the more you contribute to the positive evolution of the world. But here's where many people fall short. They limit their growth to what they think they can manage. Why? Growth can be scary sometimes. You begin to deal with hiring and management issues… even if you outsource everything to independent contractors. You may experience cash flow issues because a lot of money is going toward supporting the growth of your business. You may fear you'll be handcuffed to your laptop, working nights and weekends and missing out on your life and family.

All of these above-mentioned growth concerns are good for you, and your business. If you are faced with growth issues, it means you are doing a great job of receiving and attracting that which you have always desired. Business growth provides you with an individualized crash course in priorities, asking for help, knowing when to say "no," and everything else you've learned about in this book. Growth is the result of living the four components of a conscious business. Growth is what conscious business is all about! Growth... and the impact it has on the world.

So, as you expand your receiving mechanism, and appreciate everything that comes to you, it's important that you simultaneously plan for the growth of your business. Begin asking for help before you desperately need it. Investigate legal and tax issues associated with growth so you are prepared and proactive in these areas of your business.

One other action I recommend you take in preparing for growth is to begin setting up your conscious business to run without you. That's not a typo. Your business ought to be set up to run without you. I'm not saying your business should run without you, but that it ought to be able to. If you're the only person who knows the inner workings of your business, growth will bring you much headache and heartache. On the other hand, if you take the necessary steps to put systems in place, to train your team to take over if needed, to get the knowledge in your head onto paper and transferred to others, you again send a strong message to the Universe that you're ready to receive more and that you're ready for rapid, expansive growth.

If you're looking for a resource to help you systematize your business operations in a way that is easy and works, I highly recommend Michael Gerber's book, *The E-Myth Revisited*.

You see, when you are committed to being a conscious entrepreneur, you cannot ignore any aspect of your business, or your life. Nothing can be swept under the carpet. Consciousness is about the awareness of it all and the willingness to act according to your awareness. It's about being in alignment with what you see in your present life and what you envision for your future life. This might sound like hard work; to be aware of every aspect of your life, looking at it all with wide open eyes and taking responsibly for what you see and doing something about it. The truth is, if you think it's hard work, it will be. On the other hand, if you accept your entrepreneurial responsibility as the most valuable Divine gift you could ever ask for, you'll discover this way of living is easy, and you'll experience fulfillment in every moment, even when the moment feels challenging. There's no path in life that is quite as rewarding than a life that is lived being wide awake!

Environments Create Your Reality

Next, you'll discover how to design environments that support your success and help you maintain your highest energy. Environments shape your reality and can help you more easily (and lovingly) move through the challenging times. Taking responsibility as a conscious business owner is not a walk in the park; it takes discipline in spirit, mind, heart, and body to maintain this path. Environments have a big impact on your ability to stay engaged and continue putting one foot in front of the other.

Environments are critically important to your conscious business success because they help you stay true to what you really desire in your heart and Soul. The more positive energy you are able to hold (feeling good as opposed to feeling bad, seeing the cup half full rather than half empty), the more ease and joy you will experience on your journey. And, the more ease and joy you experience, the more the feelings of ease and joy increase.

We talked about this in an earlier chapter as it pertains to the concept of "what you think about, you bring about." Environments have much to do with the thoughts that pass through your mind, consciously and unconsciously. With the conscious awareness of setting up environments to support you, you can have a drastic positive influence on your state of being... the place from which all things are revealed. So, let's look at the different types of environments and how you can use them to support your Highest, Divine good to keep the energy flowing!

I break down environments into two categories, internal and external. Internal environments include your mindset, attitudes, and connection with Source, sense of peace, beliefs, faith, and level of trust. These are all environments that exist within you. One of your most important jobs as a conscious entrepreneur is to maintain a healthy, aligned, spacious, and joyous internal environment.

Oftentimes this requires deep personal and spiritual work to shift your state of being, so your core doesn't easily get rocked. There's a lot of information I've shared already in this book to help you on this path, so I'm going to assume that you are conscious of the need to do your personal work on the inside to help you experience a state of joyous being and manifestations on the outside.

In this chapter I'm going to focus on setting up supportive, loving, uplifting external environments that also help to support your internal environment.

Of course, the very fact that you have a conscious business is a tremendous environment right there. But there are many more environments that can be designed to support your ultimate success. Some of these have already been mentioned in other parts of this book, but for the sake of making it easy for you to have one complete resource at your fingertips, here are the environments I've used that have been a great success for me. I trust you'll resonate with at least one of them and get to work implementing it in your life right away. Remember, this final step of *The Freedom Formula* is about maintaining your energy and receiving your dreams. These external environments are designed to help you do just that.

Physical Surroundings

The physical surroundings that you exist in every day in your home, office, and car are environments that have a massive impact on you. Why? Because they are the energetic, physical space in which everything else occurs. If you are surrounded by clutter, stacks of papers that need to be filed, have bookcases that look like they belong in the thrift store and a bathroom that hasn't been cleaned in months... these are all examples of environments that do not contribute to your Highest and best good.

When you exist in less than desirable environments, a messy car for example, the feeling you have as you sit behind the wheel is pulled down because the space that surrounds you doesn't represent the Highest within you. I'm not saying that you need to live in a big home, with new furniture, drive a fancy car and hire a professional organizer. What I am saying is it's your responsibility to take care of those possessions you have (everything from your home to the papers in your file drawer) in a way that supports you.

Sometimes this will mean you give away furniture, eliminate old files that have no relevance anymore, donate a bunch of old clothes to a charity, get your car washed, or hire a housekeeper to keep your home clean. I know you know what I'm talking about here. Just think about the last time you organized a drawer, cleaned out a closet, or gave your car a detail job. Feels great, doesn't it? Because you've released stuck, cluttered energy that was making you feel stagnant and confused; it gave you more energy.

I've got one word of caution when it comes to physical environments. Do not take everything on at once. If you think of organizing and de-cluttering your entire office, it can feel too overwhelming to start. Instead, begin with one drawer, not even the whole desk. One drawer at a time, one file at a time, you will slowly but surely begin to experience a physical environment that actually supports you in achieving your goals.

Accountability Buddy

An accountability buddy is a trusted friend or colleague who cares about you, your business and your life and would like to be part of an accountability partnership to keep you both moving forward with aligned action. Once you've identified that person, simply set up a phone call with him or her every week, preferably at the same time each week. Ten minutes is all you need to schedule with your buddy.

When you hop on the phone with each other you simply state those tasks which you are committed to doing that week, those tasks you intended to accomplish the past week, and a status report of whether or not you did what you said you were going to do. You both write down what you're committing to doing the following week, and you write down what your buddy is committed to doing, too. That way, the next week when you talk, you can hold them accountable and not let them slip any undone commitments through the cracks. This is about holding each other to a standard of honesty and integrity in achieving your goals.

With that in mind, you do not have permission to beat yourself or your buddy up if they do not honor their commitment. Rather, take a look at the commitment and identify what happened that it was not realized. Maybe it became insignificant in the course of your week, maybe a fear came up around doing it, and maybe you simply procrastinated. Whatever it is, identify the reason why and either recommit to doing it, or remove it from your task list for the coming week, if it no longer serves you to accomplish it. This pertains to the section where we discussed "dumping" tasks that are no longer aligned with you. Never do something just because you said you would, if it no longer resonates with you as something worth doing.

Keep in mind that these tasks you commit to doing each week are designed to infuse you with energy and help you be your Highest and most joyous expression in the world. If they're not connected to that end goal, they are worth some serious consideration about if you should be doing them at all, or perhaps delegating them to someone else to do.

Vision Partner

A vision partner is set up similarly to an accountability buddy, except what you discuss during each weekly talk is completely different. A vision partner is someone who holds a space for you to verbally communicate the vision that is in your heart and Soul. The vision can relate to your business, your life, your book, your relationships, the dreams you want to manifest, vacations you want to take, anything that tickles your fancy and evokes an energized state of being. All you need is another conscious entrepreneur who you know, like, and trust. Having a vision partner to receive your vision and believe it for you (they need to be committed to seeing it as already done) is one of the most powerful and fun tools you have to boost your level of energy, enthusiasm and anticipation of what's yet to be revealed. Once you've found a visioning partner, make an appointment to talk on the phone for fifteen minutes every week.

When working with your vision partner, it helps to create a physical environment prior to the call to support the conversation. Light a candle, play some relaxing music (or whatever your version of creating that environment is) and allow yourself to physically relax by taking some deep breaths. Creating this sacred spaced in which to share your vision contributes to the energy that is released as you speak.

When you first establish the call, you may want to do a brief centering exercise together to align you with each other and establish the sacred space in which you'll share. Just taking a few deep breaths together can easily get you centered. (That's the former yoga instructor in me speaking.) Each of you in the vision partnership has an obligation to listen to your partner without judgment. You simply open your heart and mind to receive what they have to share as if it's absolutely, already a done deal. The person starting simply speaks his/her vision to the partner. One option is to read the vision exactly as written in the exercise, or you can close your eyes, take a few deep breaths, connect to Source and speak spontaneously, in the moment, about the vision for your life and business. As you do, the partner's job is to listen to you, hold the vision for you, and see it as absolutely already done and coming to you now. Then, switch roles and listen to your visioning partner share his/her vision and hold the space for them of seeing it already done. The experience of having another person listen to you with the intention of your vision being realized is deeply powerful. Plus, coaching someone else through their vision will provide deep insight into your own process.

I urge you to find a partner and get started with this today because it's not only fun, it works!

Mastermind Group

A mastermind group generally consists of a dedicated group of people who gather (in person or on the phone) for the purpose of supporting each other and helping each other stay on track with their goals and intentions. The most successful masterminds are ones in which the members have similar goals and dreams they're working toward. The momentum of seeing others working toward their goal helps everyone in the group rise together and make progress toward their goals too.

Masterminds where members experience the best results are those run by a thought leader/expert in the area of expertise the members require to achieve their goals. This expert is paid to lead, coach, educate, inspire and manage the group to stay on task and make consistent progress.

There are also mastermind groups that are self-selected and self-run with no designated or paid leader/expert. These groups usually do not produce the same results as the ones where a leader is paid to run the group, provide support, accountability, and foster powerful relationships amongst those involved.

Mastermind groups offer an environment that allows you to ask for support, resources, input and ideas for any challenges you may be facing on your path. These groups work best when they consist of committed, like-minded, purposeful people who believe in the power of both giving to and receiving support from the group. They also know the journey is more fun and powerful when shared with others.

A mastermind group typically meets quarterly, monthly or bi-weekly, and has more of a back and forth flow than the astute listening that transpires in an accountability buddy or vision partner relationship. This is where you get to share ideas and insights with your coach and peers, and receive valuable solutions, wisdom, insight, and support.

I have participated in and run several mastermind groups, and they are incredibly powerful environments for transformation, growth and goal achievement. It is a gift beyond words to be part of a group where you know you have trusted colleagues, and a coach, to support you toward your goals on a consistent, ongoing basis.

Circle Community

A circle community is like a spiritually focused self-run mastermind occurring generally once per month in person. In a circle, the leadership is often shared so everyone is seen as equals. The agenda for a circle typically remains consistent from month to month, and includes an opening ritual, sacred sharing and closing ritual.

Women's circles, specifically, have been around since the cave days where women gathered in circle around the campfire to support each other in their lives... mostly supporting each other to stay alive, in those times. In today's environment, women's circles are popping up in every corner of the world, for the sole purpose of supporting each of its participants in their Highest good, and the Highest good of the world. For me, personally, my circles are some of the most influential and all-sustaining environments I have in my life.

Personal Relationships

This external environment doesn't need much explaining. You know if the relationships in your life are serving you, or not. The ones that serve you infuse you with energy and cause you to have "woo-hoo" and "quiet thank you" moments. They are the relationships where you leave that person feeling better than before you interacted with him or her.

On the other hand, relationships that don't serve you feel like someone is sucking the life out of you. They drain you, draw from your light and leave you feeling frustrated, discouraged, or just plain tired. Do your best to limit these depleting, draining relationships and develop deeper relationships with people who support you, believe in you, and celebrate you!

When it comes to relationships, quality is far more important than quantity. Consider yourself blessed if you have a handful of people who really know you, see you, support you, and believe in you... and you the same for them. Better to have three supportive and deep relationships than thirty unsupportive or surface ones.

Coaching Program

A coaching program is a designed for group that meets in person or via telephone for a specific purpose and a fixed amount of time. It consists of people who pay to be in the coaching program because they want to learn something specific from the coach.

Some people join coaching programs to help them create information products, establish their brand, create a website, learn how to implement a publicity campaign, discover how to invest in real estate, how to improve their relationships, or as we do in my company to help you *Get Your Book Done*®. The options are as endless as there are coaches with information and expertise that helps others.

The important thing to remember here is to do your research and only join a coaching program with a coach who you resonate with, has a track record of success, has a high level of integrity, delivers more in value than what they charge, and cares about your success. In today's world, coaching programs are a dime a dozen. Anyone can create one. Do your due diligence and avoid being scammed by a program that over-promises and under-delivers.

Private Coaching

A private coach is someone you hire to work one-on-one with you, and only you. This type of coaching requires more of a financial investment, because the coach is making him or herself exclusively available to you.

Individual coaching formats range from a 30-minute phone conversation every week to private full-day or weekend retreats and year-long intensives. And the price tags range according to the programs. Often, conscious entrepreneurs make this type of investment in a specific coach because they know that coach has wisdom and information that can help them shift to where they want to be in their business or their life.

If you are looking for someone who will be dedicated to your success, will push you, ask you the hard questions, share their wisdom generously, and who you have a heart/ Soul connection with, then a private coach may be the perfect external environment for you.

Other Environments

These environments are just a small sample of some of the most common environments and communities that conscious entrepreneurs engage in. There are many more environments, such as your church or spiritual center, personal development groups, hobby groups, and many, many more.

It's important to remember you should never feel like you're walking your path alone. You deserve and need to be surrounded with love, support, and guidance every step of the way.

ACTION GUIDE EXERCISE #19:

Make a commitment to the environments
you'll put in place to support you.
What do you need to change,
take away, or add?

Action Guide, page 30
www.thefreedomformula.com/guide

It Takes a Village

You've heard the expression, "It takes a village to raise a baby." I take this phrase one step further to say, "It takes a village to raise a business—especially one that puts Soul in the business and money in your bank." Any dream worth pursuing can't be done alone. You'll need help along the way: moral support; a shoulder to cry on; cheerleaders to celebrate your greatest victories; and people to share their wisdom and resources with you and to believe in you if you ever lose belief in yourself. Your "village" is there to keep you on track to manifest everything your heart desires (this or something better, right?). I once heard someone say there are no self-made success stories; anyone who has become a success has made it by having a village of support around them.

Getting support is what gave me the energy I needed to take some major risks in my business, do things I never thought I could do, dream bigger than I used to dream, and keep going when it felt impossible. Having a support network around you will literally make the difference between success and failure, between a $50,000 business and a $500,000 or $5,000,000 business, between just getting by and as Oprah would say, "Living your best life!"

Maintain the Process

One of the most important things to remember on your journey of putting Soul in your business and money in your bank is to stay engaged in the process. The life of a conscious entrepreneur requires a lot of emotional, spiritual, mental, and physical energy. So, if you ever become complacent, lazy, tired, disengaged from the greater good of the universe or unenthused about evolving, transforming and growing, it's time to put at least one of the previously listed external environments into place to make sure you stay engaged in the process, and don't quit when it gets hard. Because it will be challenging at times!

And here's a bit of encouragement for those moments you do feel disconnected and disengaged from the process that's unfolding. The simple fact that you can recognize when you're disconnected is proof that you *are* connected.

In recognizing the absence of connection, you make yourself aware of connection. It is the awareness of the absence that brings forth the sense of presence. This is so important to remember, as it will be a lifeline when the going gets so tough you feel like giving up.

Another thing to keep in mind as you experience the ups and downs of the conscious evolution of you and your business is that it's impossible to fail. Anything that feels like failure isn't; it's simply a lesson offering guidance to move you forward on a more aligned path. It shows you one way things didn't work out as hoped and therefore points you closer to what will work out as you had envisioned.

Imagine yourself on a hike and you come to a fork in the trail. You're not sure which way to go, so you choose one of your two options only to realize you made the "wrong" choice. Now, it's true, you went out of your way a bit and "failed" to get closer to your destination, but the good news is now you know exactly where to go because one of your two options didn't work out.

Keep this analogy in mind for your business. You will make plenty of turns that lead you down a path that doesn't move you closer to your goals. But, each path you take, and each one that isn't "right," is there to serve your Highest good, teach you valuable lessons, offer valuable insights, bring you new relationships, new ideas and a blinking sign as to where you ought to take your next step. If that road didn't work out, you have a new opportunity to make a different choice. You simply cannot fail when you accept that failure doesn't exist; it's a disguise for the gifts of guidance, wisdom, insight, deepened faith, and personal transformation.

Persistence is Power

Conscious entrepreneurship requires persistence. As with any aspiration in life giving up doesn't serve anyone, especially you. If you are committed to living the four components of conscious entrepreneurship: making money, making a difference, being fully who you are and trusting in your Divine Path... quitting isn't an option. Let me rephrase that.

Quitting those things that no longer serve you is a good thing. But quitting on the pursuit of your Highest Self-expression isn't. Right? I quit one of my businesses because it was a considerable drain on my time, money and energy. But, quitting on that business was a necessary action in order for me to stay committed to my Highest Self. That business was weighing me down. Without it, I've been able to soar much higher than I ever would have if I had kept it going.

Persistence can be a tricky thing. You can persist forever trying to push a piece of string uphill. And, no matter how long you try, how much you intend and envision pushing that string uphill, the fact is that you can't push string uphill. It's physically impossible. If you find yourself pushing string uphill, do not persist. Put your heart, Soul and energy into a more fulfilling endeavor, one that has true potential for extraordinary results on every level of your existence.

The Highest endeavor to pursue is connecting more and more closely with the Divine spark within you. The very spark that is Life itself. Some people call that God. This unending pursuit is the kind of persistence I'm talking about.

Everything is this chapter is geared toward keeping your energy up, to keeping the "positive vibes" flowing through you in each and every moment. Expansive energy allows for receiving. Receiving helps you feel expansive. This is the continuous cycle of a conscious entrepreneur. Energy is the MULTIPLIER of *The Freedom Formula*, so please do whatever it takes to maintain your emotional, spiritual, mental and physical energy.

I talked a lot about outside support in this chapter. Outside support is something it took me a long time to embrace. I thought I had to do everything on my own. I'm not sure what it is about us humans but for some reason, many of us have patterns that make it scary to ask for help. Some people think it is a sign of weakness. I see it as a sign of great strength. It takes courage to open yourself up to the village and be accountable to a coach, teacher, mastermind group or partner. But courage moves you through fear and draws you further along your journey of freedom.

Freedom Revisited

The ultimate entrepreneurial dream is freedom—the pursuit of which invites you to face your fears, expand your vision, get out of your comfort zone and open up to let Spirit guide you to your Highest and richest expression in the world.

Think back to the beginning of this book, where I asked you to write your personal definition of freedom. Do you remember your definition? Did you want to be free from something that was weighing you down? Did you want freedom to pursue something? Whether you wanted to be free *from* something or free to move *toward* something, freedom as it pertains to conscious entrepreneurship is a process of putting all the pieces of *The Freedom Formula* together.

First, you must go inside to discover the Soul of your business… which is YOU! Then it is essential to connect with your Source as well as your market. Without the ability to connect on both levels, you will not be able to manifest the success, freedom and fulfillment you're looking for. Next, it's important to design your business; to truly create it in a way that serves your Highest expression and supports the life you want to live.

Once you design your business in the invisible/intangible realm, it's important to ground it in the physical realm. You do this by taking action in the world and continuing to move forward one step at a time. Finally, in order to continue to grow yourself and your business, you must maintain your energy (no matter what) so you can easily and gracefully realize your entrepreneurial dreams.

Putting Soul in your business and money in your bank is not a "one and done" process. Creating your business this way is a life-long journey of continual alignment, expansion, growth, evolution, realization, transformation, manifestation, understanding and success.

While there are many aspects to consider when putting Soul in your business and money in your bank, the good news is you now have the five-step formula to make it all possible.

So, I invite you to use this formula regularly. Please don't close this book and forget about what you learned when you wake up tomorrow morning. Rather, I invite you to make a commitment to yourself that you'll embrace and implement this formula from now on, so you can experience the ultimate success in your life and your business... true personal, spiritual, emotional and financial freedom!

Action Guide Exercise #20:

Revisit your personal definition of freedom
and see if your definition needs to be shifted
now after completing this book.

Action Guide, page 30
www.thefreedomformula.com/guide

Congratulations… you did it! Now, enjoy LIVING it!

**(Soul + Connection + Design + Implementation)
x Energy = FREEDOM**

AFTERWORD

~~~

The End is the Beginning

Take a look at the five steps of *The Freedom Formula* again:

- Step 1: Discover the Soul in Your Business
- Step 2: Connect to Your Source...
  and to Your Market
- Step 3: Design Your Business
- Step 4: Implement Your New Business Vision
- Step 5: Maintain Your Energy and Realize
  Your Dreams

Once you complete the fifth step of maintaining your energy and realizing your dreams, you may find yourself naturally cycling back to the beginning... and re-discovering the Soul in your business at a deeper level.

You see, as a conscious entrepreneur, your journey never ends until your release your physical body and birth into spirit. As long as you are a living, breathing creature of God walking on this earth in this incarnation, your journey will never end. Every day brings new opportunity, new insights, new understanding, new relationships, new ideas, new approaches, new wisdom… new everything.

It's about the journey, not the destination. Your responsibility now is to surrender to the journey of your conscious business, as a pure and sacred expression of who you Divinely are. And, I mean ALL of who you are. No part of your being gets to hide, no part of you gets to dim its light. Every part of you needs to be present in every moment.

Please, always continue to pursue your freedom in knowingness that once you experience a new freedom, it is a time of joyous celebration and gratitude. But, truly the greatest gift in the pursuit (and acquisition) of your goals is who you become along the way, moment by moment, experience by experience, and transformation by transformation.

I've designed this book so it has increasing value every time you read it. You can pick this book up again and again at any point in the future and have a completely new experience with it. Because the eyes with which you'll read these words next year will be different than those you read with today.

READER RESOURCES

Here are some of the most powerful programs and services that are offered through my company. I share them with you to give you some great resources to help you take the next steps with your own book, business... and life.

Private Coaching

Sometimes you need that extra level of focus, privacy and accountability – someone to be there for you on the phone, someone you can trust, someone to whom you can text and email your most pressing questions to move forward with your book, business or life. That's what this service is for. I don't do it often, and I don't work with anyone. This partnership is precious between me and my clients so I limit private one-on-one coaching to just six clients at a time and an interview is required to see if we're a fit. Request an interview by emailing info@christinekloser.com.

Got a book inside *you*? Do you want a natural, organic way to write your book so that it flows out of you effortlessly? This flagship course has helped thousands of transformational authors around the world. In fact, I used it to write this book! Its success is due to the step-by-step system that shows you exactly what to do and the order in which to do it so you can easily write your book. Get more details here: www.getyourbookdone.com.

You want to know what the biggest writing secret is among top bestselling authors? It's two words: *writers groups*. Throughout history authors have relied on a group of fellow writers to give and receive feedback, support each other and share in the joys and challenges that only other authors truly understand. *My Time to Write* is an exclusive writing group of committed, motivated and inspiring authors. We have five writing retreats a year, including one in an exotic location like Tulum, Costa Rica or Bob Marley's house in the Bahamas. Learn more and request an application here: www.mytimetowrite.com.

TRANSFORMATIONAL AUTHOR EXPERIENCE

Since 2011 I've held a virtual training where I gather top book publishers, agents, editors, marketers and bestselling authors to share their wisdom on writing, publishing and promoting books. It was at this event that the words "transformational author" were first used... and nearly 80,000 writers from 127 countries have participated. Get more details here: www.transformationalauthor.com

TRANSFORMATIONAL AUTHOR BREAKTHROUGH

This must-attend event has been praised as the most transformational, impactful, life-changing and business-building event for authors and leaders around the world. Breakthrough graduates have gone on to become bestselling authors, sign book deals, land on TEDx, appear in major media, speak around the world and grow their income... and impact! People credit this live event as the turning point that got them the breakthrough they needed to accelerate their success. Get more details here: www.transformationalauthor.com/breakthrough

CONTACT
CHRISTINE KLOSER

Address:
Christine Kloser Companies LLC
211 Pauline Drive #513
York, PA 16402

Phone:
(800) 930-3713

Email:
info@ChristineKloser.com

Website:
www.ChristineKloser.com

For bulk buys and quantity discounts of
The Freedom Formula, please call (800) 930-3713.

ABOUT THE
AUTHOR

Christine Kloser is an international speaker on the topics of transformational authorship and leadership. She has written thirteen books, including the best-selling and award-winning books, *Conscious Entrepreneurs, The Freedom Formula, Pebbles in the Pond, A Daily Dose of Love* and *Get Your Book Done.*

Throughout her career she's coached clients from all walks of life including entrepreneurs, speakers, coaches, consultants, trainers, retirees, advocates, psychotherapists, doctors, cancer survivors, wellness practitioners, community leaders, and more. To date, Christine has trained nearly 80,000 aspiring authors from 127 countries and has personally helped more than 400 of them get their books published, and into the hands of happy readers.

Many of her clients have gone on to become best-selling authors, sign traditional publishing contracts, double or triple their business revenue, and appear in major media including: *CNBC, CBS, Time, Business Week, CNN, ABC, New York Times, Animal Planet, Fox & Friends,* and more.

People experience these successes as a result of participating in Christine's powerful services and programs, including private coaching, *Get Your Book Done®, My Time to Write®, Breakthrough LIVE,* and the *Transformational Author Experience.*

When Christine isn't writing, speaking or coaching transformational authors and leaders, she can be found cooking, running carpool, on a date with her husband, soaking in the bathtub, hula hooping, reading, walking, at the spa, or on the dancefloor doing West Coast Swing.

Will You Post A Review on Amazon?
If you like what you read in
The Freedom Formula, I'd greatly appreciate
if you'd post a favorable review on Amazon.
This will help me reach more people
with this message. Thank you!
Go here to post your review:
www.freedomformulareview.com

ACKNOWLEDGEMENTS

As in any undertaking in life, it takes a tremendous amount of support to birth a book, (even an updated edition). There are so many people to thank for the contributions they made to me, both knowingly and unknowingly as I walked through the experience of birthing this book again.

To God, who has gifted me with so much to be grateful for and has given us all a Divine spark of light that can never be extinguished, no matter what. This book would never have been brought to life, had You not assisted me in writing every single word. Thank you.

To my parents, who not only gave me the gift of life but have loved and supported me every step of the way even when they didn't understand what I was doing, or why I was doing.

To all of my clients, customers, mentors, teachers, colleagues, subscribers, partners and friends for being the mirrors that help me see who I am. And, to my sacred circle of Soul sisters across the United States, thank you for your light and love.

To Laurel, Kamila, Sierra, Bonnie, Peggy and Terri for being the beta-testers of *The Freedom Formula* in 2008.

The impact you had on the first version of this book coming forth is profound. Thank you for helping the floodgates within me to open and flow from my heart to my keyboard.

To my family of transformational authors, thank you for playing such an important role in helping me step more fully into the work I'm here to do. Working with you has helped me connect more deeply with who I am and has allowed me to bring more of myself into this updated version of *The Freedom Formula.*

To my stellar team of peer reviewers, Christine, Don, Linda, Randi and Ellen - thank you for taking the time to read this manuscript and provide your honest and valuable feedback. You helped shape this book into what it is today.

To my rock star team at Christine Kloser Companies LLC and Capucia Publishing. Carrie, Jean, Colin, Kathy, Penny, Ranilo, April, and Gwen. Thank you for everything you do to support our amazing clients and keep the wheels of our company moving. You are the force that makes what we do for people around the world possible.

To my husband David, who was the first one of us to proclaim, "I'm going to write a book." If you had never stepped up to the plate to write your book, my journey working with authors would never have begun. Thank you for standing by my side through the ups and downs of life. There's nobody else I'd rather be walking this path with than you. Thank you for loving me as fully as you do and for being my greatest cheerleader, and shoulder to lean on. I love you!

And, to our daughter Janet. Thank you for your amazing laugh, brilliant mind, creative spirit, beautiful Soul and willingness to speak your voice. You are one of my greatest teachers.

And, finally, to the spirit of the child I miscarried in 2006. Your short presence in our life is a blessing beyond words. Losing you was the catalyst that caused me to re-evaluate everything and make new decisions that lead to the writing of the first edition of this book.

42551908R00116

Made in the USA
Middletown, DE
21 April 2019